AF531237

FORMATION AND TRANSFORMATION OF POWER IN RURAL INDIA

FORMATION AND TRANSFORMATION OF POWER IN RURAL INDIA

V. ANNAMALAI

1996
DISCOVERY PUBLISHING HOUSE
NEW DELHI—110 002

First Published—1996

ISBN 81–7141–323–4

Published by :

Discovery Publishing House
4831/24, Ansari Road, Darya Ganj,
New Delhi—110 002 (INDIA)
Phone : 3279245

Laser Typesetting by :

Allied Computers,
Karnal (Haryana)

Printed at :

Tarun Offset Printers,
518/14, Adarsh Mohalla,
Maujpur, Delhi-110 053

Preface

The social and political power relationships in Indian rural society have engaged the attention of social scientists for long. The explorations in power formation in rural India are largely confined to village studies where the nuances of power operation are not specifically highlighted. The need for a thorough understanding of power structure in terms of inter-relationship between sources of power and power holders in rural India, was long over due. Further, there is a need for studying new areas so as to further our understanding of power formation and to find regional variations and patterns. In addition the study aims at capturing the changes that have been taking place in the power formation in the late eighties and early nineties.

This research study resulting out of an intense field study in Pudukkottai district of Tamil Nadu examines the power formation in the rural area and tries to fill in the gap. The study set out to achieve two objectives—overlapping yet divided for analytical purposes. The first objective was to examine and analyze different sources of power to identify different power holders. For this purpose the study enquired into different sources of power like caste structure, landholding in terms of caste-wise ownership and holding size, institutions like statutory village Panchayat, Co-operatives and political parties.

The second objective was to discuss the inter-relationship between sources of power and power holders. This study explores the dynamics by analyzing the power holders over the years and their derivatives; interactions between and among the sources of power and power holders; gradual shift of social and political power to different groups; and how the changing face of rural institutions such as village panchayats and rural cooperatives, and also rural development programmes have transformed the power formation in rural India and vice versa. This research study highlights, inter alia, how the internal and external sources of power transforms the local power formation. In the absence of periodic elections to Panchayati Raj institutions and Cooperatives, the power holders with formal position in political parties emerge as a middlemen or opportunistic leaders.

The author is thankful to a number of individuals wno have made this work possible and a reality. Everyone of them spared their time and extended a helping hand in their own way. First of all I am thankful to Mr. P. Vanamali, Deputy Director General, NIRD for his encouraging words about the present work. I am also thankful to Mr. D. Sathyamurthy, Registrar, NIRD for having gone through the work and made useful suggestions.

I would be failing in my duty if do not acknowledge the keen interest shown by Dr. S. P. Jain, Director, Centre for Panchayati Raj in my work and insisted on getting it published it at the earliest. I gratefully acknowledge all the help extended by Dr. R. R. Prasad, Director, Centre for Social Development in more than one way. My thanks are also due to my colleagues Dr. K. R. Sastry and Dr. K. Jayalakshmi for their help.

In the field, P. Murugasen needs a special mention here for all the help he rendered to me. I am equally thankful to K. Nammalwar, whose discussions and insights about the area had gone into the writing of the work. My heartfelt thanks to Osci, Prithivi, Balu and other members of "Kudumbam" for making my long stay in the field a pleasant and enjoyable experience. My thanks are due to my friends Sunil B. Ray, N.G. Satish, Oommen John, Gangi, Prakash, Krishnamurthy, Srinivasan and Suman Chandra with whom I had many hours of discussion.

My friends Satish, Ramachandar, Raj Kumar and Bhumaya in the Computer Centre have been very helpful in many ways. I am thankful for the typing assistance given by Mr. Muralidhar and Varman and for maps to Mr. Subha Rao.

Finally my thanks to all my family members including my mother Maragathammal and my sons Adithan and Arunodhayan for their help in their own way during the course the present work.

V. Annamalai

Contents

Preface V

1. Theoretical and Methodological Framework 1

2. Pudukkottai District : A Profile 25

3. The Village and Its People : Towards Understanding the Milieu 54

4. Sources of Power : An Analysis 87

5. Power Holders : Their Profile and Sources of Power 113

6. Transformation of Power 134

7. Conclusion 157

Bibliography 163

Index 177

Theoretical and Methodological Framework

INTRODUCTION

Indian rural society had been the subject of discussion by British administrators, scholars from different disciplinary background and Indian nationalists since the beginning of the nineteenth century. In recent years, a large number of village studies have been conducted by anthropologists, economists, political scientists, and sociologists. These studies have resulted in critical appraisal of earlier views and conceptions about Indian rural society. These studies, conducted across the country, have brought out rich empirical material and have also shown the underlying uniformity across regions as also regional variations.

One aspect of rural society which has engaged the attention of academics in the recent years is power formation and its dynamics. Notable contributors to the subject, apart from others, are Bailey[1], Beteille[2], Gough[3], Harriss[4], and Srinivas[5]. Some deal directly with the phenomenon of power in rural areas taking it as one of the variables studied. Others have contributed to the related aspects of power formation like dominant caste, leadership, factionalism, etc.

These studies also comment upon the nature of power formation in terms of distribution of power and shift of power from one section of population to the other in the changed context of adult franchise and party politics, and various institutions like Panchayati Raj and Co-operatives.

Though these studies have commented upon the phenomenon of power, exclusive attention has not been paid to the inter-relationship between the sources of power and power holders. Hence the need for studying sources of power to understand which person(s) has/have what source(s) of power and how shifts or changes in sources of power affect power holders.

Further, there is a need for studying new areas so as to enhance our understanding of power formation and to find regional variations and patterns. In addition to this the study aims to capture the changes taking place in the power formation in the eighties and in the early ninetees.

THEORETICAL FRAMEWORK

This section firstly discusses the concept of power in terms of its definitions and applications. Further, the relevant literature is reviewed to highlight the findings of other scholars and to identify gaps, if any, in them. Against this background the significance of the present study is stated and its objectives are defined.

POWER : DEFINITIONS AND APPLICATIONS

There are many concepts used in the present study, however, the concept of power is central one as the research focuses on its formation and dynamics. Power, like other related concepts such as influence, authority etc., has many definitions and so also their applications. Different definitions of power by scholars have been critiqued on methodological and theoretical grounds. The following section attempts to draw broad contours of the debate centred around this concept.

Broadly speaking, power as defined by various scholars refers either to characterise a capacity or to a relationship. When it refers to capacity it is the capacity to affect the actions of others or impose ones own will on others. In this context let us take up two well known formulations on power and analyse them.

For Weber "Power is the probability that one actor in a social relationship will be in a position to carry out his own will despite resistance regardless of the basis on which this probability rest."[6] For Dahl power means "A has power over B to the extent that he can make B to do something that he would not otherwise do".[7]

There are certain similarities in these definitions. Firstly they assign power to individuals rather than to institutions or to entire societies. However, some sociologists like Parsons and Poulantzas disagree on this point.

For Parsons "Power is generalised capacity to secure the performance of binding obligations by units in a system of collective organisation, when the obligations are legitimised with reference to their bearing on collective goals and where in case of recalcitrance there is a presumption of enforcement by negative situational sanctions—whatever the actual agency of that enforcement."[8] According to Poulantzas "Power is the capacity of a social class to realise its specific objective interests."[9]

Both Parsons and Poulantzas view power as essentially a structural property manifest in an entire society rather than its constituent individuals.[10] Thus, the former tends to attribute power to individuals while the latter to social and collective relationships.[11]

Secondly, apart from individualistic orientations in definitions of Weber and Dahl, there is another similarity which is the of capacity of persons to impose a will on other persons despite resistance. However, Parsons argued that Weberian definition assumes conflict and antagonism in the process of exercise of power. It ignores the possibility that power relations may be relations of mutual convenience[12]. This criticism is also applicable to Dahl's definition of power which also has the element of conflict built into it. Hence, power relations should be viewed as not only in antagonistic terms but also in mutually convenient terms.

Though there are certain similarities in the definitions of Weber and Dahl, there are differences as well between them. Weber defines power positively in the sense of enacting one's will.[13] This is in tune with Russell's definition of power as "the production of intended effects"[14] and the modified version by Wrong who treats power "as the capacity of some persons to produce intended and foreseen effects on others"[15]. In Dahl's definition, on the other hand, power is primarily negative in so far as it is identified foremost with another person's will. However, this may not necessarily be the same as carrying out one's own will.[16]

Another difference between these two definitions is that while overcoming the resistance is a secondary feature in Weber's definition in effect becomes the primary and the exclusive element of Dahl's definition.[17]

From the above analysis of different conceptions of power by scholars it is evident that while some emphasise on individualistic aspect and others on structural aspect of power,some interpret power relations in terms of conflict and others in terms of consensus. While some conceptions of power emphasise on imposing ones will or affecting others behaviour despite resistance the others emphasise on willing compliance.

The definitions discussed above are narrow in scope because of their emphasis on some aspects of power while ignoring the other aspects. The present study sought to define the concept of power in a much more comprehensive manner. The study defines power as a capacity of person or persons or groups to affect others behaviour with or without resistance in a system of social relationship, institutional framework and socio-economic structure.

The study views that individual power is to a large extent dependent on institutional power. It is within the institutional framework that the individuals or power holders acquire power.[18] Thus, the conception of power proposed by the study gives primary emphasis to the institutional bases of power exercised by different power holders.

The concept of power is not only varied in its definition but also in its application. Different conceptions of power advanced by sociologists and political scientists, particularly in the United States have resulted in their adoption of different approaches to the study of power. This has given rise to what has come to be called as 'community power debate' between elitist and pluralist.

Some scholars, on the one hand, who believe in elite model described American political life as being governed by a relatively coherent elite. Opposing this view is a group of scholars who believe that the plural model of countervailing power groups spread over desperate issues is the one which characterizes American political life.[19]

Walton has noted that sociologists have tended to identify power structures as basically 'elitist'. They have largely depended on reputational method to identify the most influential people in the community.[20] This method was first used by Floyd Hunter in his study of community power structure in Atlanta City, Georgia.[21] The methodology adopted was to compare the lists of the people deemed most influential by the people chosen as judges then tally up the score for each person named to arrive at those thought to be powerful. In this way he identified forty key individuals as those who recurred across the different judges' estimates. Hunter called these people local community political elite. The group, as Hunter found out, was not composed randomly but was heavily weighed towards business interest and found out pyramidical power structure.

This approach to the study of community power has been criticised for many reasons. One of the major criticisms, according to Clegg, is that " the reputational approach makes power equivalent to the average of some specifically chosen people's perception of it. What these people think power is may not accord with what it ` really' is, assuming that there is a reality to power outside people's perceptions of it."[22] Similar criticism expressed by Polsby[23] who points out that the reputational method relies on the second hand opinions instead of studying the behaviour of the power holders.

Political scientists, however, have favoured decision making method. This approach involves the study of key decisions covering number of preselected issue areas. Those who successfully initiate or oppose key decisions are then regarded as the most powerful members of the community.[24] The notable contributors of this method is Dahl,[25] Polsby,[26] Wolfinger[27] and Jennings.[28]

The central method used by Dahl in his study 'Who Governs' was to determine for each decision which participants had initiated alternatives that were finally adopted, had vetoed alternatives initiated by others or had proposed alternatives that were turned down. These actions were then tabulated as individual successes or defeats. The participants with the greatest proportion of successes out of the total number of successes were then considered to be the most influential.[29] In short, according to Polsby, in the pluralist approach "an attempt is made to study specific outcomes in order to determine who actually prevails in community decision making".[30] The stress is on the study of concrete, observable behaviour.[31] The researcher, Polsby feels, should study actual behaviour either at first hand or by reconstructing behaviour from documents, informants, newspapers and other appropriate sources.[32]

The decision making method, like reputational method, has been subjected to criticism. Major criticism, particularly of decision making conception of power has emanated from Bahrach and Baratz who coined the term non-decision making.[33] The crux of their criticism lies in the proposition that the study of power must not only focus on decisions but also non-decisions. They quote Schattschneiders in support of their view that all forms of political organization have a bias in favour of the exploitation of some kinds of conflict and the suppression of others because organisation is the mobilisation of bias. Some issues are organised into politics while others are organised out.[34]

Both the methods as propounded by Dahl and Barach and Baratz try to identify power through the analysis of the actual outcomes of decision or non-decision making. They have provided a viable alternative to the earlier reputational approach. This alternative enabled them to examine more closely the powers that be and not just the power that people think there is.[35]

Both the reputational and decision making methods, however, were criticised by Lukes as one and two dimensional views respectively.[36] Firstly, these approaches have the bias of methodological individualism which places the focus of power processes on a series of individually chosen acts instead of locating it in the "socially structured and culturally patterned behaviour of groups and practices of institutions". Lukes argues that a more adequate view of power should consider the many ways in which manifest and potential issues are being influenced, through the operation of social forces and institutional practices. He calls this view as a three dimensional view of power.

Another criticism by Lukes against both the views is that they have associated power with-and only with-the presence of observable conflict of interest.[37] However, his conception of power says: A may exercise power over B by getting him to do what he does not want to do but he also exercises power over him by influencing, shaping or determining his very wants. Indeed is it not the supreme exercise of power to get another or others to have the desires you want them to have, that is, to secure their compliance by controlling their thoughts and desires? By shaping or determining the desires and wants of the community no issue would ever arise in the first place and consequently there is no need to resort to non-decision making. The power which is there now work through the consensual values which it has created. In this third dimensional realm of power, no resistance needs to be overcome because resistance has been removed.[38]

Thus, both reputational and decision making approach to study community power structure have proved to be limited in their applications. The former emphasises on second hand opinion of what people think power to be may not accord with what it really is. The latter tends to emphasise on the behavioural conception of power by treating power with its actual exercise and confining themselves to its manifestations.

The studies which employed these methods have located power holders on the basis of their reputation or their role in decision making. They, however, have neglected on their base or source of power which make it possible for them to exercise power [39] The present study, therefore attempts to place greater emphasis on sources of power thereby locating power holders. In other words different sources are to be studied so as to identify who has what source of power. There are two underlying assumptions to the approach. Firstly, it is the various sources of power which enable the power holders to exercise the same. Secondly, the emphasis on the sources of the power holders presupposes that subjects lack these resources and that the inequality in control over resources is the basis of the power relations.[40]

Thus, the present study examines various sources of power to identify power holders. In this context, the research conducted on power formation in India is reviewed as a background to the present study.

RELEVANT STUDIES : A REVIEW

Many village studies have been conducted with different disciplinary backgrounds enquiring into various aspects of Indian villages like caste, class, Panchayati Raj, Co-operatives, religion, politics etc. While some studies focused on the social and economic structures, culture, religion and institutions in the villages, the others dealt with the changes brought about by the outside forces. These studies helped in broadening our understanding of the macro-level and micro-level realities as well as inter-relationship and interactions between these two levels. Further, these studies highlight the regional diversities in terms of local structures, processes and histories.

Among these studies, there are some which focus directly on power formation and its dynamics and others not dealing directly with power formation as a central focus of their enquiries, but provide valuable insights into the power related issues like leadership, dominant caste, factionalism, patron-client relationship etc. The studies which focused on power formation either solely or as one of its many aspects of enquiry have not come to an agreement on the nature of power formation, the different sources of power and the changes in the sources of power that effect power holders.

Beals in his study on the changing leadership of a Mysore village found that there was movement away from social hierarchy and caste domination to more liberal and democratic tradition.[41] In 1952, while age, heredity and wealth continued to be important in determining social position,the dominant class in the village was a middle class group of educated small businessmen, farmers, teachers and factory workers. The emergence of new leadership was attributed to the increasing education and close proximity of the village to a large city. This group which had been educated in schools, where English and Gandhian ideals of democracy and social equality were taught, placed little faith in traditional ideals of caste and social stratification. Beals has noted that this educated new middle class is the power holder in village though they had to face the attack once in the wake of famine by the village Patel-a village headman chosen by the Government on the basis of heredity. During this time village Patel attempted to assert the superiority of his caste and to pronounce himself the supreme authority in the village. However, Patel lost in the struggle. Thus, Beals study shows that there is a shift in power holders and that the role of rich landowners, priestly castes and money-lenders has come to an end in the village.

Bailey in his book "Caste and Economic Frontier : A Village

in Highland Orissa " reveals that power has shifted from upper caste to lower caste and it is no longer monopoly of one segment of the community but it is dispersed.[42] He feels that the shift in power has occurred because of changes in the economy and recognises the economic changes since the coming of British administration in 1855 to the village. He observes two fold changes in the village economy viz., (a) Coming of land into the market (b) Commerce, trade and jobs entering the village economy. Before 1855 political power and wealth were concentrated in the hands of upper caste There have been changes in the distribution of lands among various castes because of the breakdown of the joint family system and the coming of commerce, trade and jobs to the village. Thus, the shift in wealth has affected the political structure of the village.

Singh observed in his study on changing patterns of stratification system in six villages of Uttar Pradesh that the upper castes (Rajputs, Brahmins and Bhumiars) and classes (ex-landlords and money-lenders) continue to hold power in villages.[43] He showed that the key offices of village President and Vice-President in almost all the six villages are with the upper castes. The class background of these elected leaders reveals similar trend of upper class domination in various offices. Further these villages continue to be deeply affected and determined by the pattern of economic deprivation and privileges of the various castes and classes. The power system has a tendency to incline in favour of the groups who can control the expectations of the people in villages.

Beteille has found out from his study in Thanjavur village in Tamil Nadu that power has shifted much more decisively from Brahmins to non-brahmins.[44] Earlier Brahmins were the landowners and monopolised political power. The political power has shifted to non-brahmins whose strength lies in their numerical superiority and political connections. Ownership of land as the basis of power is less decisive, he feels in acquiring power. According to him, these new bases of power are, to some extent, independent of both caste and class.

Beteille concludes that in addition to economic superiority acquired from the Brahmins the capacity to patronise lower castes is now vested with the non-brahmins. This gives them a following and also numerical strength which are necessary for sustaining power. Like Bailey, Beteille has demonstrated that power has shifted from upper to the middle castes. Further he states that the lower castes are yet to benefit from this power transformation.

Bhatt in his study enquires into the inter-relationship between caste, class and political power.[45] He observes that before independence there was close relationship between all the three variables and most of the power holders were from upper caste and class. He has pointed out that the situation has undergone changes. The study demonstrated that an individual's socio-economic and political life today is not entailed by his caste position in any significant measure.

Sinha in his study of two villages in Bihar found out that in one village wealth, caste and age continue to be sources of power and the same set of individuals continue to hold power despite introduction of adult franchise, election, community development programmes and elected village councils.[46] In another village it was found that power is not a clear mark of wealth, caste and information. In this village it is evident that change taking place from "status to contract" and this is largely result of accelerated communication facilities, adult franchise election, party organisation and wider political linkages.

Sharma establishes that the upper castes possess the maximum extent of total village land.[47] According to him although there is monopolisation of land by a few families of upper caste, the political development taking place is going against their interest day by day. He has noted a tendency for competition in the Gram Panchayat elections since 1955 instead of unanimous elections. He observes that as the contest will increase, the importance of unanimous election will decrease. He concludes that because of this trend the domination of upper caste will decrease.

Harris in his study of a village in North Arcot district in Tamil Nadu found that non-brahmin caste is controlling not only lands but also informal and formal Village Panchayats.[48] They had also come to occupy important positions in political parties at the local level.

For Oommen the castes which are numerically superior as well as economically dominant are politically the most powerful, if they are not divided into competing factions.[49] Even if a caste is numerically insignificant its economic importance will facilitate the capturing of a number of positions in what he calls "power pool".

Sheer numerical superiority of a caste will facilitate the recruitment of at least a few members into the power pool, even when the caste is economically underprivileged and ritually depressed.

Oommen classifies the power wielding groups into three distinct categories: (a) those who derive their source of legitimacy from tradition. (b) Those who occupy positions in organisations introduced in the context of development activities and active political workers and (c) those who have reputation for certain personality attributes, particularly ethical qualities.

The studies reviewed above touches the nature of power formation in terms of distribution of power and also shift of power from one section of population to the other in the wake of introduction of adult franchise and party politics and also introduction of various institutions to facilitate development. In a majority of the villages studied various scholars have shown that power formation has been undergoing changes across the country. Though these studies have contributed immensely to understand power formation in rural areas there are a few gaps in these studies.

NEED FOR THE STUDY

Though the studies reviewed above have commented upon the phenomenon of power, exclusive attention have not been paid to the inter-relationship between the sources of power and power holders. Hence, the need for studying sources of power to understand which person(s) has\have what source(s) of power and how changes in sources of power affect power holders.

The studies also show that there are certain similarities and also variations in the power formation within regions which makes the task of generalisation difficult even at regional levels. Even within Tamil Nadu variations are noted in the sources of power, shift in the importance of these sources and its impact on the power holders. There is also shift of various powers from one group to another. This necessitates conducting an inquiry on different region to broaden the base of understanding. Accordingly, Pudukkottai district of Tamil Nadu was selected where study of this nature has not been carried out.

Secondly, studying a new region helps in comparing the findings with that of other scholars who did research on power formation and its dynamics in rural areas.

Lastly, though the present research is a case study of a Panchayat village it is hoped that it will contribute towards understanding the regional diversity and also will help in theory building at macro-level.

OBJECTIVES OF THE STUDY

The present study attempts to achieve two objectives-overlapping yet divided for analytical purposes. The first objective is to explore different sources of power and analyse these sources giving rise to different power holders. In other words it attempts to identify which power holder/s has/have what source/s of power. For this purpose, different sources of power like caste structure, landholding in terms of caste-wise ownership and holding size, institutions like statutory Village Panchayat, Co-operatives and political parties have been examined.

The second objective is to probe and analyse the interrelationship between sources of power and power holders. This involves studying of the process of acquisition and exercise of power by different power holders, changes in the sources of power and their impact on power holders.

The following section explains the methodological framework for collection and analysis of data to achieve the above mentioned objectives.

METHODOLOGICAL FRAMEWORK

The methodological details of the study are as follows : types of data collected and their sources, process of data collection and analysis, organisation of the study and the limitations of data collection and analysis.

(A) TYPES OF DATA AND THEIR SOURCES

The study of this nature necessitates mainly collection of qualitative data. However, quantitative data was also collected, whenever it was felt necessary and relevant, as a basis for or as a support for qualitative data. For instance, the landholding details of various landowners in terms of caste and category were collected from revenue records of the Panchayat. This served as a basis for understanding and validating qualitative responses. The study also elicited qualitative responses to cross-check the quantitative data on landholding, agriculture and irrigation, etc.

There have been debates in the recent years about the strength and limitations of qualitative and quantitative data collection and analysis. While some scholars view them as antagonistic, others view them as complementary.[50] According to Patton quantitative and qualitative methods involve differing strengths and weaknesses, they constitute alternative, but not mutually exclusive, strategies of research. Patton feels that both qualitative and quantitative data can be collected in the same study.[51] Thus, the present study views both the types of data as mutually complementary rather than antagonistic in nature. In the study, however, primary emphasis is laid on collection of qualitative data because of the nature of the study. The collection of qualitative data involves detailed description and indepth enquiry into the phenomenon under study.[52] Accordingly a descriptive account of various aspects of the phenomenon of power in rural areas is presented. Further, qualitative data is supported by direct citation of respondents' personal comments, views, perspectives and experiences.[53] According to Bryman, "many qualitative researchers prefer to employ verbatim quotations from interviewees' replies in order to illustrate general points".[54]

Both the qualitative and quantitative data have been gathered from primary and secondary sources. The primary sources include interviews, individual and group discussions and observations. For this, the researcher met a cross section of people so as to get a representative picture of the situation under study. The cross section of respondents included persons from various castes of all social ranking, landowners with different landholdings, agricultural labourers, petty shop owners, artisans, women and youth.

Apart from these persons, officials of various departments from village to district levels and persons from the voluntary organisations working in the area were also interviewed. Prominent persons from the adjacent villages were interviewed to strengthen the data derived from the respondents of the Panchayat. Further, certain key informants were also selected on the basis of their access to confidential information, their trust in the researcher, and their knowledge of the past history of the village and the area. The researcher also stayed in the area for many months where he had chance to observe certain events like village and family festivals, disputes between different persons or groups etc.

The secondary source covers gathering of relevant materials from books, articles, journals, newspaper clippings and so on. Secondary data was also collected from the district Gazetteers, land records of the revenue village, census reports and government publications which include annual reports of various departments. These were useful in collecting data on agrarian condition particularly on land holding, cropping pattern, agricultural seasons, level of mechanisation of agriculture, agricultural labour and irrigation, economy, population, caste groups and structure, results of assembly elections, Acts of and information on Panchayati Raj, Co-operatives and various rural development programmes.

B) PROCESS AND METHODS OF DATA COLLECTION AND ANALYSIS

The data collection and analysis was done in many stages. In the first stage, based on the emerging trends in the existing literature, broad theoretical areas to be enquired into were identified. During that stage it was decided to take up the study in Pudukkottai district of Tamil Nadu. This is the region where no indepth analysis has been carried out. In addition, the researcher belongs to the same cultural milieu. This helped not only in the process of data collection but also in analysis. Further, earlier experience of the research in various projects particularly 'Farmers Agitation in Tamil Nadu' conducted in the northern part of Tamil Nadu has been utilised not only in the initial stage but through out the study.

In the next stage, a Panchayat village comprising of cluster of hamlets was identified and selected for the inquiry. In the selection of the Panchayat (a) a Panchayat with population range of 1500 to 2500 and (b) multi-caste composition were taken into account. The criterion of population was based on census report of 1981. In the census report it was mentioned that in Pudukkottai district most of the villages fall within the population range of 1500 to 2500. Additional reason for identifying the Panchayat of this range was that the village under enquiry should not be too large for a single researcher to cover in view of the constraints of time and resources available. At the same time it should not be too small to have a meaningful coverage. The purpose of selecting village with multi-caste composition is to have castes from various social ranking and to capture the complexity of power.

Adopting these criteria and with the help of friends working in the Kulathur taluk of the district, several villages were identified for possible selection of the sample Panchayat. The researcher also had discussion with block level officials to get an idea about different Panchayats. With the required background information the researcher visited various Panchayats for selection.

Some villages were rejected as they had large or small population. Some villages were rejected on the ground that they were mainly inhabitated by either a single or a few castes without all the social rankings. Finally, Udayallipatti Panchayat consisting of a main village and five hamlets was selected. In 1981 its population was around 1800. It is a multi-caste village occupied by castes of all social rankings with persons from upper level castes-mainly cultivators, middle level castes-artisans and service castes and lower level castes-agricultural labourers.

At this stage of field work secondary data for the Panchayat in particular and the area in general was collected. Data on the Panchayat includes details of agriculture and irrigation, occupational classification, Panchayat elections, Co-operatives, electoral list etc.,were collected. Apart from these details secondary data was also collected for block and district levels to provide background to the study. The process of collection of secondary data and identification of the Panchayat took fifteen days.

With the help of secondary data about the Panchayat, block and district, the researcher could acquire a broad picture of various aspects of the district in general and the Panchayat in particular. This helped in sharpening the issues to be inquired into regarding power formation and its dynamics. Further, having identified the issues for inquiry, questions-with some close ended and others open-were designed to make the interviews flexible.

The second stage of field work involved staying more than three months in the study area. The primary data was collected through semi-structured and indepth interviews, group discussions and observations. Before elaborating on these techniques of data collection, it is necessary to discuss about the selection of respondents for interview.

From the electoral list(1986) of the Panchayat population, different caste groups were identified and listed with the help of local persons. In this way nineteen caste groups were listed. There were 1337 voters living in 379 households in 1986. Subsequently key informants were identified and interviewed for the purpose of eliciting descriptive accounts of the various aspects of the Panchayat. Further, by using snowball sampling method they were in turn asked to identify their friends and relatives with whom the interviews could be held.[55] To get representative picture of the situation, the researcher interviewed a cross section of the respondents in terms of caste, occupation, landholding, age, gender, and youth. Data on socio-economic background of power holders was also collected not only from other respondents but also from the power holders themselves.

As mentioned above, three research techniques were used mainly for collection of the primary data. The foremost among them is semi-structured in-depth interviews. This strategy was adopted based on the earlier research experience in applying standard and formal questionnaires which leave little flexibility in eliciting sensitive information and probing into further details. Though questionnaire has the advantage of easy analysis by quantification, it imposes a preconceived and rigid design on the social reality. Semi-structured interview method, on the other hand, employs a set of themes and topics to frame questions for the purpose of interview. This strategy by now is familiar to the students of qualitative research. Apart from flexibility in its design it allows the process of enquiry to probe the unexpected which cover up issues which are difficult to envisage at the stage of questionnaire finalisation.

With the tentative questions a few of the respondents were interviewed. The emphasis in these interviews was to get descriptive accounts of various aspects of phenomenon under study. After a few interviews, areas of enquiry became more focused and question became more precise the main line of enquiry, the researcher tactfully brought back the process of interview of the desired direction. This process yielded not only descriptive but also rich and indepth data.

The interview data were collected using more than one method. (a) Tape recording the interview (b) taking notes on the interview as it progressed and writing a full report later and (c) making notes after the interview. The different methods used in this context were dependent on the situation. For instance tape recorder was used whenever the respondents showed enough of trust and were willing to go on record. One of the advantages of using this method was that interviews could be conducted without disruption. Another advantage with the method is that the recorded interview could be preserved and that the exact words of respondents could be retrieved. This may not be possible in the conventional method of making notes after the interview. The disadvantage with the method is that some people might not like to go on record on certain matters like landholding, corruption, local politics and so on. Faced with the situation the researcher resorted to either taking notes during the course of interview of after the interview was over.

Simultaneously group discussion method was also adopted to elicit primary data. These were conducted generally in tea shops where people assemble frequently and also during the time of village festivals. The researcher used to initiate discussion on various relevant topics and issues to elicit various view points. This method was not only useful for generating fresh data but also to cross check the data gathered through other methods.

To supplement these techniques obervation method was also used. This method is generally known in anthropology and sociology as participant observation method. This has been employed to study Indian villages even by eminent sociologists.[56] In this technique of data collection the researcher may have to be active and at times passive.[57] Gold[58] has devised four ideal types of field roles: the complete participant, the participant observer, the observer as participant and the complete observer.

On the participant observation method Burgess remarks that the extent of participation can change overtime.[59] In some cases the researcher may begin as an onlooker and gradually becomes a participant as the study progress of vice versa. The researcher during his stay in the village, depending on the context played either the role of a complete participant or a complete observer. For instance in the village festivals the researcher did participate completely. In certain instances, the researcher chose to maintain an onlooker's position. For instance, during the quarrels among the people the presence of the researcher was always noted. An interventioin would have affected the situation.

Alongwith these methods of data collection the field notes were taken everyday. The field notes consisted of recording of events, situations and conversations in which the researcher involved. It also consisted to the observations and comments of the researcher. These notes were classified under different themes. These were complimentary to data gathered through other methods.

To make the data more reliable and to cross-check the data gathered through other methods, certain informants were contacted frequently. These individuals were selected for frequent contacts as they had reposed trust in the researcher. They were also useful in getting confidential and sensitive data which were otherwise difficult to collect from other respondents.

Apart from these data, case studies were also collected. The case studies related to family disputes, inter-caste quarrels, disputes regarding temple affairs, land disputes and factional fights so on. These were useful additions to the existing data. These also helped in understanding the role of power holders in settling the disputes.

Data about the other Panchayats were also gathered so as to compare and cross validate the observations on the Udayallipatti Panchayat. Data gathered particularly included caste groups, landholding pattern, caste background of Panchayat Presidents and Chairmen of various co-operatives.

The use of multiple methods for investigation has not only helped data collection but in validation of data as well. The process of triangulation of methods has also helped in generating reliable data.[60]

Secondary data were collected at this stage of field work particularly land records of Udayallipatti Panchayat which is also a single revenue unit. This process of secondary data collection was carried over several field visits as information sought was not readily available.

After the field work both quantitative and qualitative data was processed. Tables were formulated to consolidate quantitative data covering aspects of agriculture, population, households and voters, Panchayat and assembly election results. Land records were analysed for nearly 1500 landowners in terms of caste and categories of landowners.

Regarding qualitative data, recorded interviews were transcribed and classified under broad themes and sub-themes. Further, data gathered through other methods were also added to the existing data. The broad themes and sub-themes, classified are caste groups and structure, landholding in terms of caste and categories of landowners, informal 'Ur' panchayat and formal statutory village Panchayat, co-operatives, education, religious activities, role of political parties, and tentative identification of power holders.

The purpose of the classification was to bring under broad themes and sub-themes various responses of the respondents and to find patterns for analytical treatment.[61] On the basis of the classification of responses, a report of the provisional findings was prepared. This report was given to experts for their comments. This helped in grounding the findings and identifying the gaps in data collection. This also in turn generated analytical questions to be posed at the next stage of field work.

The next stage of field work stretching over two months was conducted primarily for filling up gaps in the collected data. Some additional persons were interviewed to clarify the provisional findings. Analytical questions were also posed to respondents for deeper understanding of various aspects of the phenomena under enquiry. The provisional findings were also discussed with some of the key respondents in the process of validation of the data. The disagreements were duly recorded and taken into account in the final analysis.

The remaining data gathered during the last stage of the field work was integrated into the analytical framework. Findings of other scholars regarding power formation and its transformation were also compared to find out variations and commonalities among these findings.

LIMITATIONS OF THE STUDY

Since it is a study of one Panchayat, drawing generalisations is difficult and premature. Howerver, attempts have been made to collect data on other Panchayats of the Panchayat Union to compare and consolidate the findings.

Other limitations of the study flow from the paucity of time and resource at the disposal of the researcher. Though it was conceived as a case study, collection of details on land transactions over the years, income and expenditure of the households could have contributed in terms of depth to the study. However, these could not be done in view of constraints like time and resource available to the researcher.

ORGANISATION OF THE STUDY

The first chapter discusses about the theoretical and methodological framework of the study. In the section on theoretical framework concpet of power in terms of its definitions and applications, as it is central to the study, is discussed. Further, the existing literature is reviewed to highlight the findings of other scholars and to identify gaps in them. Significance and objectives of the study are also stated in the theoretical framework.

Though the present work is a study of a Panchayat village it was necessary to have a broad picture of the area in which the Udayallipatti Panchayat is located. This would help in highlighting the similarities and variations between the broader area and the sample Panchayat. Hence second chapter presents various features of Pudukkottai district like position and topography, agriculture and irrigation population characteristics, Panchayat system, Co-operatives, performance of political parties.

Though broader contours are drawn in the earlier chapter it is important to sketch the local milieu as it provides for an indepth understanding of the various features of the Udayallipatti Panchayat. The third chapter, hence, gives descriptive account of the study Panchayat.[62]

Fourth chapter focuses on various sources of power so as to identify power holders and their sources of power. Fifth chapter, on the other hand, sketches and compares the profile of various power holders and their sources of power.

The mere identification of power holders and comparison of their profiles may not be sufficient for understanding power formation and its dynamics. It was necessary to probe into the inter-relationship between power holders and their sources in terms of changes in sources affecting various power holders. The sixth chapter is devoted to study the inter-relationship between sources of power and power holders. The last chapter summarises the findings of the study.

NOTES AND REFERENCES

1. F.G.Bailey, *Caste and Economic Frontier : A Village in Highland Orissa* (Manchester : Manchester University Press, 1957).
2. Andre Beteille, *Caste, Class and Power : Changing Patterns of Social Stratification in Tanjore village* (London : University of California Press, 1965).
3. Kathleen Gough, *Rural Society in South-East India* (Cambridge : Cambridge University Press, 1981).
4. John Harriss, *Capitalism and Peasant Farming : Agrarian Structure and Ideology in Northern Tamil Nadu* (Bombay : Oxford University Press, 1982).
5. M.N.Srinivas, *The Dominant Caste and Other Essays* (Delhi : Oxford, 1987).
6. Quoted in Stewart R. Clegg, *Frameworks of Power* (New Delhi : Sage, 1989), p.73.
7. Ibid, p.51.
8. T.Parsons, *Sociological Theory and Modern Society* (New York : Free Press, 1967), p.308.
9. N.Poulantzas, *Political Power and Social Classes* (London : New Left Books, 1973), p.104.
10. Barry Barnes, *The Nature of Power* (Chicago : University of Illinois Press, 1988), p.6.
11. Dennis H.Wrong, *Power : Its Forms, Bases and Uses* (Oxford: Basil Blackwell, 1979), pp.673-81.
12. Roderick Martin, *The Sociology of Power* (New Delhi : Ambika, 1978), pp.36-38.
13. Sik Hung Ng, *The Social Psychology of Power*(London : Academic Press, 1980), pp-36-38.
14. Bertrand Russells, *Power : A New Social Analysis* (London : Unwin Books, 1960), p.2.
15. Dennis H. Wrong,op.cit., p.2.

16. Sik Hung Ng, op.cit., pp.103-104.
17. Ibid.
18. Murali Manohar Sinha,*Community Power Structure in Rural India : A study of two villages in Bihar (India)* (New York : Unpublished thesis from Cornell University, 1979), pp.5-6.
19. Stewart R. Clegg, *Power, Rule and Domination : A Critical and Empirical Understanding of Power in Sociological Theory and Organisational Life* (London : Routledge and Kegan Paul, 1975), pp.17-18.
20. J.Walton,"Substance and Artifact : The Current status of Research on Community Power Structure ", *American Journal of Sociology* 71, pp.430-438, 1966.
21. F.Hunter,*Community Power Structure* (Chapel Hill : University of North Carolina Press, 1953), p.5-6.
22. Stewart R. Clegg, op.cit., p.50.
23. N.W.Polsby,*Community Power and Political Theory* (New Haven : Yale University Press, 1963), pp.50-51.
24. Stewart R. Clegg, op.cit., p.17.
25. Robert A. Dahl, *Democracy and Power in an American City* (New Haven : Yale University Press, 1961).
26. N.W.Polsby, op.cit.
27. R.E.Wolfinger, *Readings in American Political Behavior*, (Englewood Cliffs : Prentice Hall, 1970).
28. M.K.Jennings,*Community Influentials : The Elites of Atlanta* (New York : Free Press, 1964).
29. R.A.Dahl, op.cit., p.336.
30. N.W.Polsby, op.cit., p.113.
31. Steven Lukes, *Power : A Radical View* (London : Macmillan, 1974), p.12.
32. N.W.Polsby, op.cit., p.121.
33. P. Bahrach and M.S.Baratz,"The Two Faces of Power" *American Political Science Review* 56, pp.947-52, 1962.
34. Ibid, pp.947-952.

35. Sik Hung Ng, op.cit., p.108.
36. For detailed criticism of both reputational and decision-making methods see Steven Lukes, op.cit., pp.11-20.
37. Ibid, p.23.
38. Sik Hung Ng, op.cit., pp.109-120.
39. Dennis H. Wrong, op.cit., p.124 and Barry Barnes, op.cit., p.8.
40. Dennis H. Wrong, op.cit., p.125.
41. Alan R. Beals, "Change in the Leadership of a Mysore Village" in M.N.Srinivas, *India's Villages* (Bombay : MPP, 1985), pp.147-160.
42. F.G.Bailey, op.cit.
43. Y.Singh,"The Changing Power Structure of village Community : A Case Study of six villages in Eastern UP", in A. R. Desai, *Rural Sociology In India* (Bombay : Popular Prakashan, 1969).
44. Andre Beteille, op.cit.
45. A.Bhatt, *Caste Class and Politics* (New Delhi : Manohar, 1975).
46. M.M.Sinha, op.cit.
47. S.S. Sharma, *Rural Elites in India* (Jalandur : Sterling, 1979).
48. John Harriss, op.cit.
49. T.K.Oommen, *Social Structure and Politics : Studies in Independent India* (Delhi : Hindustan Publishing Corporation, 1984).
50. See for detailed discussions on quantitative and qualitative methods in social research Alan Bryman, *Quantity and Quality in Social Research* (London : Unwin Hyman,1988), Bruce L.Berg, *Qualitative Research Methods for the Social Sciences* (Boston : Allyn and Bacon, 1984) and A.L.Strauss, *Qualitative Analysis for Social Scientists* (Cambridge : Cambriage University Press,1984).
51. M.Q.Patton, *Qualitative Evaluation and Research Methods* (New Delhi: Sage, 1990), pp.13-14.

52. Ibid, p.40.
53. Ibid.
54. Allan Bryman, op.cit., p.48.
55. For details of snow ball sampling method see Robert G.Burgess, (ed), *Field Research : A Source Book and Field Manual* (London: George Allen and Unwin, 1982), pp.75-78 and Robert.G.Burgess, *In the Field : An Introduction to Field Research* (London : Unwin Hyman, 1989), pp.54-56.
56. M.N.Srinivas, op.cit., pp.14-17.
57. M.S.Schwartz and C.G.Schwartz, "Problems in Participant Observation", *American Journal of Sociology* Vol.60, No. 4, pp.343-53.
58. Quoted in Robert G.Burgess, op.cit., pp.80-85.
59. Ibid.
60. For a discussion on triangulation of methods see Robert G. Burgess, op.cit., pp.143-167 and Bruce L. Berg, op.cit., pp.4-6.
61. For classification and analysis of data see Robert Burgess(ed.), op.cit., pp.235-238.
62. The use of study Panchayat or study village refer to the Udayallipatti Panchayat.

Pudukkottai District : A Profile

I

Historical background, physiography and ecology, population characteristics, agriculture, irrigation and industrial development, caste groups, rural institutions such as Panchayat system and Co-operatives and electoral politics of the district are the features enumerated in this profile. The profile of the district is not elaborate as it only intends to give a general picture of the broader milieu in which Panchayat village under study is located and also to show the similarities and variations in the features between the district and the Panchayat under study. The coverage is based on secondary data. Some data given are for earlier years as the latest figures for all the aspects of the district are not available. With these limitations the present chapter is attempted.

The section on the history of the district provides a bird's eye-view of the district from 15th century to the present day. The physiography and ecology deal with the physical features of the district which include the terrain, rivers, climate, etc.

The population characteristics cover such aspects like sex ratio, rural and urban distribution, SC population and literacy rate. The feature on agriculture and irrigation shows the types of soils, cropping pattern and seasons land use, landholding pattern, occupational pattern of the population engaged in agriculture and different irrigation sources. These features of agriculture are compared with the state level trends to show the similarities and variations. This section also deals with the industrial development of the district. Caste composition of the district is drawn on the basis of the 1931 census to show the numerical strength of different castes. Other relevant aspects of different caste groups are also discussed.

The rural institutions such as Panchayati Raj and Co-operatives are also elaborated in terms of its history in the district, various Acts enacted concerning these bodies, present structure, powers, functions and finances of these bodies and about the elections to these bodies. Performance of the political parties in terms of seats won is also presented to show the strength of various parties in different constituencies of the district, particularly Kulathur Assembly constituency, in which the study area is located.

Pudukkottai district is one of the smallest districts in Tamil Nadu with an area of 4,661 Sq. kms. and a total population of 11,56,813 persons living in 747 villages and eight towns as on 1981. The district lies between latitudes 9.50-30N" and 10.44'and longitudes 78.-25-5"E and 79.-16'13. It has borders with Thiruchirrapalli in the north, Thanjavur in the north-east and with Pasumpon Muthramalingam and Ramanathapuram Districts in the south (see map.I) The district is divided at present into seven taluks, viz.,Kulathur, Thirumayam, Alangudi, Arantangi, Pudukkottai, Gandarvakottai and Avudaiyarkoil.

HISTORICAL BACKGROUND

Pudukkottai, the district where the study Panchayat is located, has a long history. The Princely state of Pudukkottai - which comprised the present day Alangudi, Kulathur and Thirumayam Taluks - did not acquire the separate geo-political entity until the late 17th Century. Before the 15th century this tract was the junction of various rival dynasties including Pandyas, Cholas, Pallavas which tried to achieve supremacy in the south. Since the 15th century, with the decline of Pandya-Chola configuration, this area passed through many hands including the Mughals. In the late 17th century, it came under the rule of Thondaiman Kings[1] Since

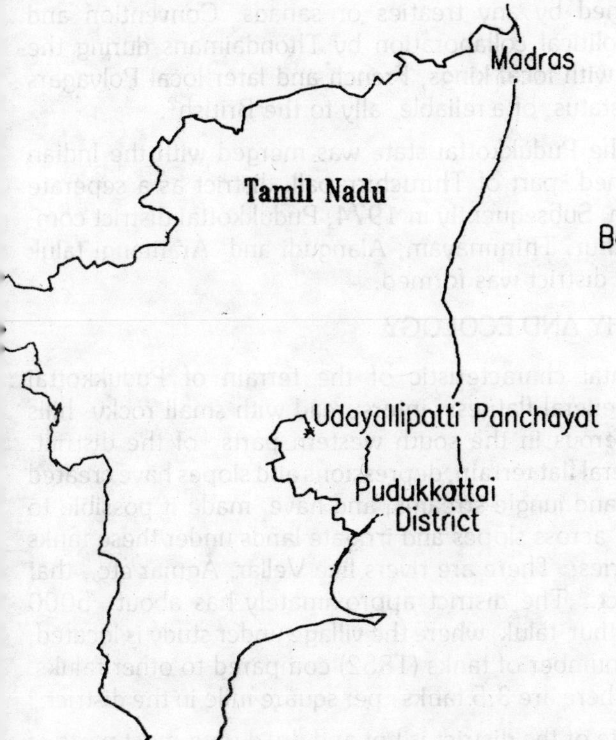

Map 1 : Location of Pudukkottai district and Udayallipatti Panchayat

then, the Thondaiman kings, belonging to Kallar caste ruled the Pudukkottai state for almost nearly two centuries till 1948. There were five Princely states under the control of the Governor of Madras during the British rule. Of the five only Pudukkottai state was not governed by any treaties or sanads. Convention and mediation of political collaboration by Thondaimans during the wars of British with local kings, French and later local Polyagars gave them the status of a reliable ally to the British[2].

In 1948 the Pudukkottai state was merged with the Indian Union and formed part of Thiruchirrapalli district as a seperate revenue division. Subsequently in 1974, Pudukkottai district comprising of Kulathur, Thirumayam, Alangudi and Arantangi taluk from Thanjavur district was formed.

PHYSIOGRAPHY AND ECOLOGY

Fundamental characteristic of the terrain of Pudukkottai District is the general flatness, interspread with small rocky hills which are numerous in the south western parts of the district. Within this general flat terrain, depressions and slopes have created seasonal rivers and jungle streams, and have made it possible to construct tanks across slopes and irrigate lands under these tanks for many centuries. There are rivers like Vellar, Agniar etc., that drain the district.[3] The district approximately has about 5000 tanks. The Kulathur taluk, where the village under study is located, has the largest number of tanks (1852) compared to other taluks. On an average there are 3.5 tanks per square mile in the district.[4]

The climate of the district is hot and dry during most parts of the year. In coastal areas of the district the intensity of the heat is mitigated to some extent by sea breeze. The average annual rainfall in the district during this century is around 940 mm.[5]

II

AGRICULTURE, IRRIGATION AND INDUSTRIAL DEVELOPMENT

Agriculture and its allied activities continue to be dominant activities of the district's population. Under broad classification there are two main types of soils i.e. red and black soil. The former is preponderant in the district. These soils are in turn sub-divided and named differently in different localities. The Pudukkottai

Gazetteer, describing the soils, says that the productivity of the tract in general is low because of the poor irrigational nourishment and soil erosion.[6]

The main wet crop of the district has been paddy. The dry crops include varagu and pulses. Groundnut has also thrived on the soils of the district. Ragi, Cholam and Cumbu have joined the dry crops of the area. Garden Crops are Maize, Tobacco, Chillies, Vegetables and Fruit crops are Mango, Plantains and Jack.[7]

There are broadly two seasons for cultivation of various crops. The summer cultivation or 'Kodai velamai' commences in the months of February - March ending July - August. The 'Kala Velamai' which is more extensive, normally begins in July - August and extend over four to six months. This seasonal rhythm depends on rainfall.[8]

Though agriculture dominates the economy of the district, the extent of its cropping is less than that of state average. The table 2.1 highlights the land use pattern for the district and the State for the year 1983-84.

While the extent and intensity of cropping in the district is less than the state average, landholding pattern in the district shows the predominance of small farmers compared with the state average (Table 2.2).

The table 2.2. gives a comparative picture of the Pudukkottai and Tamil Nadu about landholding size, operational holdings (percentage) and area operated in each (percentage) category.

The distinct feature of the district regarding landholding is that under category holding size below 0.5 hectares percentage of total number of operational holding is nearly 63 while the state average for the same is nearly 49 percent. The table 2.3.gives the occupational pattern in the district in 1991.

Grouping the Main workers by categories in terms of Cultivators and Agricultural Labourers is shown in the Table 2.4.

In the year 1971 cultivators constituted 57.91 percentage and Agricultural labourers 19.91 percentage of the district. However, in the year 1981, the cultivators constituted 55.68 percent and Agricultural labourers 20.90 percent. In 1991 the cultivators constituted 48.60 percent and Agricultural labourers 25.85 per-

Table 2.1: Land use pattern for Pudukkottai and Tamil Nadu (1983-84)

S. No.	Particulars	Percentage	
		Pudukkottai	*Tamil Nadu*
	Total Geographical area (in sq.km)	4,66,329	1,29,94,243
1)	Forests	5.09	15.62
2)	Barren & uncultivable land	2.10	4.43
3)	Land put to non-Agril. use	27.29	9.80
4)	Cultivable waste	2.89	2.43
5)	Permanent pastures & other grazing lands	1.15	1.66
6)	Land under miscellaneous crops and groves not included in the net area sown	0.31	1.41
7)	Current fallows	14.51	12.60
8)	Other land fallows	3.93	4.46
9)	Net area sown	42.72	44.99
10)	Area sown more than once	3.22	8.46
11)	Total cropped area	45.93	53.45

Source : Annual Statistical Abstract of Tamil Nadu, 1983-84, Department of Statistics, Madras, pp. 66 and 70.

cent. It is clear that while percentage of cultivators has declined the percentage of Agricultural labourers has increased during these twenty years.

A comparative statement of Pudukkottai district and Tamil Nadu as a whole in 1991 in terms of different category of workers reveal some interesting features.

From the Table 2.5 it might be inferred that the district has distinctly higher percentage of cultivators 23.76 percent more than Tamil Nadu as a whole. In Agricultural labour category, the state figure is 8.78 percent higher than that of Pudukkottai.

The district distinguishes itself in irrigation as well. Irrigational requirements of the district are met by tanks, rivers, canals and streams as surface water and wells- both open and bore- as sub-surface water. A marked feature of the district in general and Kulathur Taluk in particular is the presence of a large number of tanks totalling approximately five thousands.[9]

Table 2.2 : Landholding pattern for the District and the State (1981)

(In Percentage)

S. No.	Holding size (Hectares)	Total No. of Operational Holdings		Area Operated	
		Pudukkottai	*T. Nadu*	*Pudukkottai*	*T. Nadu*
1.	Below 0.5	62.73	48.74	17.71	10.66
2.	0.5 to 1.0	18.41	21.00	17.30	14.07
3.	1.0 to 2.0	11.31	16.81	20.74	22.18
4.	2.0 to 3.0	3.69	6.26	12.19	14.28
5.	3.0 to 4.0	1.55	2.89	7.43	9.35
6.	4.0 to 5.0	0.84	1.57	5.21	6.62
7.	5.0 to 7.5	0.82	1.58	6.74	8.87
8.	7.5 to 10.0	0.31	0.59	3.68	4.68
9.	10.0 to 20.0	0.27	0.45	4.85	5.52
10.	20.0 to 30.0	0.04	0.06	1.36	0.74
11.	30.0 to 40.0	0.02	0.02	0.83	2.13
12.	40.0 to 50.0	0.05	0.01	0.41	0.27
13.	50.0 & above	0.05	0.01	0.41	0.27
		100.00	**100.00**	**100.00**	**100.00**

Source : Census of India 1981.

Table 2.3 :Taluk-wise occupational pattern of the district in 1991 (To total population in percentage)

Taluks	Main Workers			Marginal Workers	Non-Workers
	Cultivators	*Agri. Labourers*	*Service H. hold etc.*		
Kulathur	21.85	11.87	9.46	5.29	51.53
Pudukkottai	21.77	10.38	7.66	6.30	53.89
Alangudi	21.64	12.19	5.95	5.75	54.50
Thirumayam	21.10	10.60	7.60	6.73	53.97
Arantangi	23.15	13.89	4.99	7.59	50.39
Avudaiyarkoil	21.05	7.18	9.04	5.63	57.09
Gandarvakottai	22.67	15.08	4.63	6.61	51.02
Dist.Ave.	**18.93**	**10.07**	**9.95**	**5.31**	**55.75**

Source : Census of India, 1991.

Table 2.4 : Main workers by categories in 1991

(In percentage to total main workers)

Taluks	Cultiva-tors	Agricultural Labourers	Service House Hold Industry and Other Workers
Kulathur	50.62	27.48	21.90
Pudukkottai	54.69	26.06	19.25
Alangudi	54.44	30.65	14.90
Thirumayam	53.66	26.98	19.36
Arantangi	56.00	33.02	11.88
Avudaiyarkoil	56.49	19.26	24.25
Gandarvakottai	53.49	35.58	10.93
Dist.Average	**48.60**	**25.85**	**25.55**

Source: Census of India , 1991.

Table 2.5 : Comparative statement of different categories of workers in 1991.

(In percentage)

Categories of workers in total Population	Tamil Nadu	Pudukkottai
Main Workers	40.82	38.94
Marginal Workers	2.50	5.31
Non Workers	56.68	55.75
Percentage of main workers by categories		
i) Cultivators	24.84	48.60
ii) Agricultural Labourers	34.63	25.85
iii) Household Industries etc.	40.52	25.55

Source: Census of India, 1991.

The tanks in the district are of two kinds : those that get water from the intermittent floods in the large streams and those that merely intercept surface water from the upland catchment area. The irrigation tanks of second type are generally linked in a series. Each tank, except the just one above in a series, besides intercepting local drainage, is fed by the overflow of the one immediately above it and feed in turn the one immediately below it.

The capacity of the tanks differ widely in terms of command area and duration of irrigation. Some of the tanks situated at the foot of the hills and endowed with springs, when supplemented with rains, ensure adequate supply of water for raising two crops or more. However in most of the areas in the district, the stored water is just sufficient to support one crop of paddy.[10] The table 2.6. gives an idea of capacity of tanks in different taluks of district.

Table 2.6:Capacity of tanks in terms of Ayacut Area in 1983

Taluk	Tanks (no.)	Ayacut area (hec.)	Ave. Ayacut Area per tank (Hect.)
Arantangi	531	22,253.04	41.91
Alangudi	503	10,976.52	21.82
Kulathur	1,852	20,614.98	11.13
Thirumayam	1,526	19,699.59	12.91
Pudukkottai	533	6,894.82	12.92
District	4,945	80,438.95	16.95

Source : Pudukkottai Gazetteer, Madras : Government of Tamil Nadu, 1983, p.317.

It is to be noted that while Kulathur Taluk has the highest number of tanks, it has the least average ayacut per tank compared to other taluks in the district.

The net area irrigated from different sources in the district is given in Table 2.7 :-

Table 2.7 : Irrigation by different sources in 1984-85

	Tanks	Wells	Govt. Canals	Tube Wells	Others
Pudukkottai	84.48	7.70	7.63	0.19	-
State	30.83	31.33	33.03	4.01	0.77

Source : Annual Statistical Abstract of Tamil Nadu, Department of Statistics, Government of Tamil Nadu, 1984-85, p.72.

Thus tank irrigation constitutes the major source of water for cultivation in the district. In fact, the district stands highest in the state as for as tank irrigation is concerned. The irrigation wells come second to meet the irrigational requirements of the district.[11]

The district is not industrially developed and the three taluks viz., Kulathur, Alangudi, and Thirumayam have been declared as industrially backward area by the State Government. There are both large and small scale industries in the district. The large scale industries are mainly engaged in areas of textiles and chemicals. The small scale industries are engaged in wood work, tinkering, fabrication of metal products, printing and binding, manufacture of agricultural implements, manufacture of cement products, automobile servicing and repairing and safety matches. In addition to small scale industries, there are a number of village and cottage industries. Prominent among them are pottery, blacksmithy, carpentry, small lime kilns, small brick kilns, basket making rope making and synthetic gem cutting.[12]

III

POPULATION

In 1991, the district had a population of 13,271,48 out of which 49.86 percent were males and 50.14 percent females. Out of the total population 85.65 percent lived in the rural areas and 14.35 percent in the urban areas, while the corresponding state average is 65.85 percent and 34.15 percent respectively.

In 1991 the average scheduled caste population of the district was 16.82 percent while the state average was 19.18 percent. The literacy rate in 1991 was 49.70 percent for the district and 54.31 percent for the State. As compared to other taluks Kulathur taluk had the lowest literacy rate, i.e. 39.60 percent and the highest being Arantangi with 51.31 percent.

CASTE COMPOSITION

With the help of census figures for 1931 we may have a general idea of present day composition of various Caste and Religious groups in the district, excluding Arantangi. The figures of 1931 present caste-wise details since 1931, caste-wise census are discontinued. Out of total population of 4,00,694 in 1931, total number in each caste, religious group, and its percentage to total population is given in table.2.8 and in pie graph 2.1.[13]

The Table 2.8. shows that Valayars were the largest caste group in 1931 constituting more than fourteen percent of the population. Next to Valayars, Kallars also had significant presence nearly twelve percent. However, Mukkulathor—Kallars, Maravars and Agamudayars—were sixteen percent of the population more than two percent of Valayars. The Scheduled caste—Pallars, Paraiyars and Chakkiliars—were ten percent. All other castes constituted less than seven percent each. Muslims and Christians constituted nearly four percent and five percent respectively.

Table 2.8 : Caste composition of the district in 1931

S. No.	Caste and Religious Group		No. of Persons	Percentage to total Population
1.	Kallar	Mukkulathor	46,743	11.60
2.	Ahamudaiyar		11,416	2.85
3.	Maravar		5,617	1.40
4.	Valayar		56.607	14.13
5.	Brahmin		11,769	2.94
6.	Vellalar		16,761	4.18
7.	Chettiar		20,438	5.10
8.	Kammalar		14,416	3.59
9.	Idaiyar		25,251	6.30
10.	Pallar	SC	24,921	6.22
11.	Paraiyar		15,633	3.90
12.	Chakkiliar		1,024	0.25
13.	Udayar		12,408	3.10
14.	Urali		9,578	2.34
15.	Muthiriyar		8,001	2.00
16.	Ambatar		5,052	1.26
17.	Vannar		4,309	1.08
18.	Kosavar		4,970	1.24
19.	Other castes		72,826	18.17
20.	Muslims		15,194	3.79
21.	Christians		17,960	4.48
	Total		**4,00,694**	**100.00**

Source : Census of India, 1931.

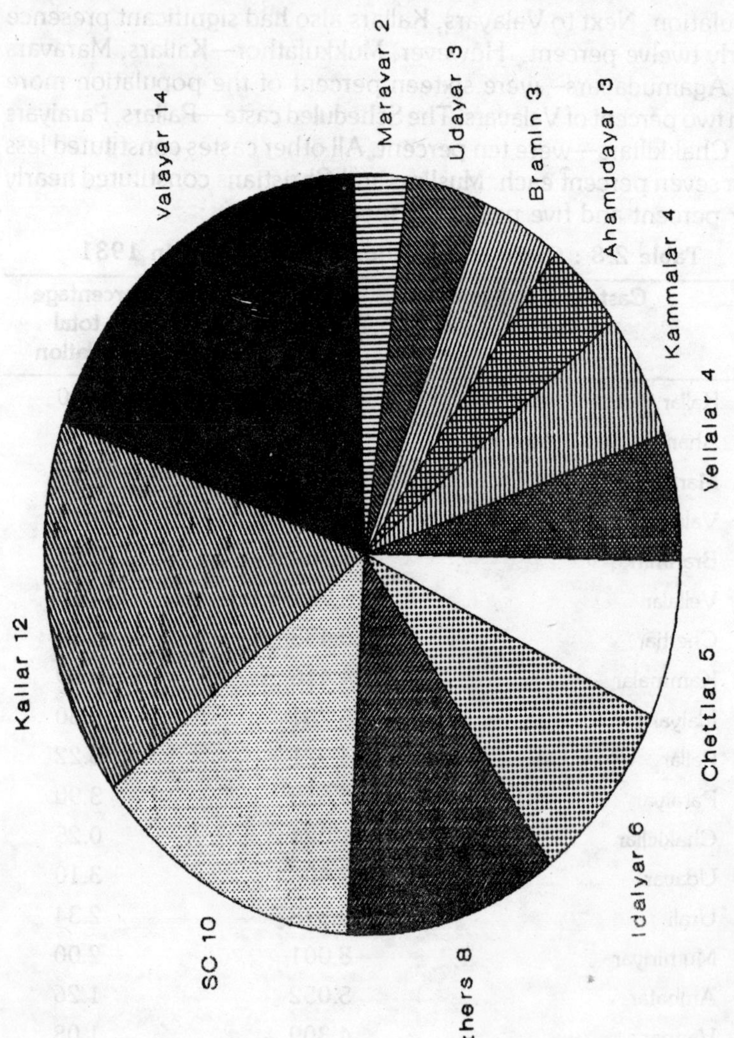

Graph 2.1 : Caste Composition of the District in 1931 (in percentage)

CASTE GROUPS

After having seen the numerical strength and proportion of important castes in Pudukkottai district, this section discusses about various features of different caste groups. It is necessary to discuss these features as this would present a broader picture of the caste groups of the district. Further, though there are regional variations but there are similarities between caste groups in the Panchayat and in the district. It is also useful for the purpose of the study to understand the interaction of castes between village level and above. The discussion is restricted only to those castes which are present in the study area. Even for those, features which are relevant to the study such as territorial divisions, kinship network, traditional occupation and caste association, if any, and general comments by different authors on different caste group, are only covered in this section. However a brief description of the castes is also made to give a complete picture.

KALLARS

Among different castes in the district Kallars form a numerically significant group. The word 'Kallar' means ' thief' in Tamil. They were described in Sangam literature as thiefs, and branded as criminals by the British. However, they were the royal caste in Pudukkottai State. The British branded them as criminals in some areas and in others they were treated as landed gentry for imitating Vellalars—a cultivating caste. In Pudukkottai State they were exempted from this mode of colonial classification because they had been set apart by the special status given to the Princely State.[14]

Kallars in the district are grouped into a number of endogamous sections called 'Nadu', a word that can be interpreted as group and also as territory or country. There were around fifty such nadus in the Pudukkottai state which included Ambu Nadu from which the then ruling family of Thondaiman came. Veesinga Nadu, a broader nadu within which fall Vadamalai Nadu (the Udayallipatti Panchayat under study belongs to this nadu) and Thenmalai Nadu etc.[15]

Before agriculture became their main occupation, the Kallars of the area earned their livelihood in two ways viz., 'Thuppukuli' system and 'Kaval' system. In Thuppukuli method, cattle is lifted by Kallar bands and returned to the owner through a Kallar intermediary on payment of half its value. In Kaval system the Kallars obtained from villagers a certain fee as an insurance against theft by Kallar bands.[16]

Kallars are part of the 'threesome' or 'Mukkulathor' community consisting of Kallars, Maravars and Agamudiyars which are numerically stronger in the old Pandya region - the present Tirunelveli, Madurai, Ramanathapuram, Thiruchirrapalli and Pudukkottai districts. Though they do not inter-marry they have caste association called Mukkulathor Association.[17]

UDAYARS (NATTAMAN)

Udayars are known otherwise as Nattambadis which literally means villagers. The Census report of 1901 gives the number of Udayars as 855 and of Nattamans as 11,160, while 1911 census gives the number of Nattamans as 12,814, without maintaining as a seperate caste. Nattamans are only a sub-division of the Udayars. The Thiruchirrapalli Gazetteer observes that Nattamans and Udayars are identical and with Malaimans and Sudramans are endogamous sub-division of one and the same caste.[18]

Udayars are sub-divided into exogamous division called 'Kanis' or fields which are named after place where their ancestors were supposed to have lived.[19] They have no regular caste panchayats unlike Kallars, and are described as frugal and very industrious agriculturists.[20]

Udayars have caste association called 'Parkava Kulam' Association which includes Surithimar, Nathamar, Malayamar, Moopanar and Nainar.[21]

VALAYARS

The term Valayars is said to have been derived from 'valai' meaning net because they originally netted game in the jungles. They are divided into several endogamous sections of which the important are the Valuvadis, Saraku Valayans, and Veda Valayans.[22] Their usual titles are Ambalakaran, Vedan, Servai. However, in the study area they are called Pusaris and officially called as Muthurajas. The traditional occupations are snaring birds, fishing, agricultural and manual labour, and collecting medicinal herbs and honey.[23] The Valayars have caste association called Muthurajas Association. The Valayars were often found in the villages on the periphery of forests in the eighteenth and nineteenth century.[24]

Valayars population in Pudukkottai in 1931 was 56607 which was more than that of Kallars. According to Dirks, the Valayars were, after Pallars and Paraiyars, the most widely dispersed. However, neither they were dominant nor did they hold extensive land rights in any locality. They were below all the other castes,in the social hierarchy but for Pallars and Paraiyars.[25]

Valayars have been listed as backward class since 1913 and were included in the list of most backward classes in 1957. Valayars as a class are at the bottom of the most backward classes in every respect. The difference between Valayars and SCs is exceedingly thin and in some areas, even partial untouchability is practised against them.[26]

PALLARS AND PARAIYARS (SCs)

Pallars and Paraiyars are the Scheduled Caste widely spread and have significant presence in the district.[27] Like Kallars they are also organised into territorial divisions i.e, Nadus. Like Valayars their settlements are spatially excluded from the upper castes settlements. They have been associated with lands for long time as agricultural labourers and as experts in determining disputed field boundaries.[28] In the study area only Paraiyars are present and not Pallars.

KAMMALARS

Kammalar is a general name given to the five occupational craftsmen viz., Thattan (Goldsmith), Kamman (Coppersmith), Thacchan (Carpenter)Kal Thacchan (Stonemason) and Kollan (Blacksmith). They claim themselves to be desendants of five sons of Vishwakarma and hence style themselves as Viswa Brahmins.[29] They have a caste association called Vishwakarma association. In the study area they are referred generally as 'Asaris'.

IDAIYARS

The Idaiyars in the study area are called Konars. Idaiyars, traditionally have been shepherds. They are generally worshippers of Lord Krishna and are thus Vaishnavites. They are divided into a number of 'Karais'. The members of each Karai have the same tutelary deity. They are said to be divided into eighteen sections.[30]

OTHER CASTES

There are other castes represented in the district and the local level. There are servicing castes like Ambatar (Barber) and Vannar (Washermen). The Vannars and Ambatars are locally referred as'Egali' and 'Navithar' or 'Maruthuvar' respectively.[31] Most of these caste people have their own caste associations. Vannars have 'Salavai Thozhillalar' Sangam and the Ambattars have 'Maruthauvakula Sangam' or'Navither Sangam'depending upon which traditional occupation they are pursuing. They are officially classified as the most Backward Classes.[32]

There are also other castes which had significant presence in 1931. These include the Brahmins including those of Tamil and Telugu origins, Chettiars, a merchant and money lending caste and Vellalars, a cultivating caste.[33] A few families of these castes were earlier present in the study Panchayat. Excepting two families of Vellalars others have now left the village. Maravar and Agamudayar though are not present in the study area, they are found in other parts of the district.

OTHER RELIGIOUS GROUPS

In 1931, Muslims and Christians formed nearly four and five percent of the total population respectively. Muslims in the district are Sunnis and most of the Christians belong to Roman Catholic denomination in Pudukkottai State. In 1981, Christians and Muslims constituted nearly five and seven percent of the population respectively.[34]

IV

RURAL INSTITUTIONS

Panchayat System

In the Pudukkottai state, which excluded Arantangi Taluk, five Union Panchayats were established under the village conservancy regulation No. IV of 1909, which was the first step towards establishing Panchayat system. Subsequently, in 1925, Pudukkottai Village Panchayat Regulation was introduced. In 1925-26 only three Village Panchayats were established. The village Panchayat

Regulation was introduced. In 1925-26 only three Village Panchayats were established. The village Panchayat, however, did not make much headway in the state as there were only 40 Panchayats out of which 38 functioned in 1946-47. The conservence of the villages which had no Union or Village Panchayat, which formed the majority, was controlled by the Revenue Department.[35]

The Madras Local Boards Act 1920 was extended to the district in March 1949 which deemed the Unions and Panchayats constituted before merger as the ones constituted under this Act.[36]

The Arantangi Taluk, which was earlier part of Thanjavur District, shared the institutions of Panchayats created in the Madras Presidency, under the Madras Act XI of 1930, Arantangi had a seperate Taluk Board which was abolished in 1934. There were several Village Panchayats in the Taluk just before Independence.[37]

After independence the Madras village Act of 1950 was introduced. At present the Panchayati Raj structure in the district is based on Tamil Nadu Panchayats Act of 1958 andTamil Nadu District Development Councils Actof1958.[38] These two Acts combined together envisaged three tier structure in which District Development councils are at the higher level, Panchayat Unions in the middle level and Village Panchayats at the lower level.

The District Development Council is purely an advisory body and do not have any executive or legislative functions. The Chairman of the District Development Council is the District collector (Ex-officio Member). Some of the non-official members are Presidents of Panchayat Union councils, MLAs and MPs elected from the various constituencies of the District,etc.[39]

The Panchayat Union is conceived of as a federation of Village Panchayats with the Presidents of Village Panchayats as members of the Panchayat Union Council. Earlier the members of the council elected among themselves a Chairman and a Vice Chairman. Since 1970 the Chairman of the Panchayat Union Council is elected directly by the voters of the Panchayat Union. Further, from 1986 elections to this post, political parties are allowed to put up their candidates with party symbols in the Panchayat elections.[40]

The areas of Panchayat Unions were made co-terminus with

development blocks established under the community development programme. The Panchayat Union Council is a governing body headed by its Chairman. In Tamil Nadu, at block level there are two block development officers—one for administration and another for development (ABDO) work under this council. The BDO is the Commissioner of the Panchayat Union who is the Executive authority of the Panchayat Union Council. Under these two BDOs there are six Extension Officers (EOs) working in different areas : Co-operation, Panchayat, Social Welfare, Social Forestry, Education and Adi Dravidar Welfare. Below EOs there are Rural Welfare Officers (earlier called Gram Sevaks) working as multi-purpose workers.[41]

The Village Panchayat and Town Panchayat represents the lower tier of the Panchayat system. The Village Panchayat Board consists of members elected from wards with seats reserved for women, SCs and STs. The Village Panchayat President is an executive authority. Till 1970 President and Vice-President were elected by members themselves. Since 1970 while Vice-President continues to be elected indirectly, President is elected directly by the voters as in the case of members of the ward.[42] Though the state Government made a move to conduct election for the post of President on party lines it was later withdrawn without assigning any reasons.[43]

The Panchayats Act of 1958 provides for Village Panchayats and Panchayat Union both obligatory and discretionary functions and in addition the functions entrusted to them by the state government. All developmental works and programmes are executed through Panchayat Union Councils. The Panchayat Unions and Panchayats are together in-charge of implementing developmental programmes. The Panchayat Union utilises Village Panchayats as its agencies for execution of development programmes at village level.

The Village Panchayats have obligatory functions including lighting of public roads and public places; construction, repair and maintenance of all village roads, bridges, culverts, road dams and causeways in such roads; construction of drains and the disposal of drainage water and sullage; cleaning of streets; provision of latrines; opening and maintenance of burial and burning grounds; sinking and repairing of wells; excavation, repairs and maintenance of ponds or tanks and the construction and maintenance of water works.

The discretionary functions of the Village Panchayats are planting and preservation of trees,lighting of public places and roads other than built up areas, opening and maintenance of public markets, cart stands, cattle sheds, public landing places, reading rooms, library centres and centres for imparting social education; establishment and maintenance of wireless receiving sets; and construction of works of public utility.

The Village Panchayats are also vested with administrative functions like administration of properties vested with Panchayats; passing of its budget and farming bye-laws; levying taxes issuing licences; executing Kudimaramathu; appointing Panchayat employees and exercising control over them and giving administrative sanction to all Panchayat works. Apart from these functions, the village Panchayats are to do the functions transferred from the Panchayat Union council from time to time.

The Panchayat Unions have obligatory functions which include construction and maintenance of public roads which are classified as Panchayat Union roads, establishment and maintenance of public dispensary, maternity and child welfare centres; construction and maintenance of houses for the poor and orphanages etc.; opening and maintenance and expansion of elementary school, prevention of any epidemic or malaria; control of fairs and festivals; veterinary relief; opening and maintenance of public market; details regarding births and deaths; and improvements of agriculture and cottage industries.

The discretionary functions of the Panchayat Unions involve undertaking measures other than obligatory functions, public utility to promote the safety health, comfort or convenience of the inhabitants of the Panchayat Union. Apart from that the Panchayat Unions are also entrusted with the execution of rural development programmes.

The Panchayat Unions have administrative functions which are management of movable and immovable properties, passing the budget, levying local charges, making periodical review of progress of implementation of the programmes and administrative sanction for such works. Further,there are certain functions transferred from agencies of the government subject to such regulations and restrictions as prescribed.

The powers and functions provided to Village Panchayats and Panchayat Unions varied from time to time since 1958.[44] For instance, after 1981, functions regarding Agriculture, Animal Husbandry, Education and Public Health were taken over by the Government from Panchayat Unions. However, in 1989 the functions like Agriculture and Animal Husbandry have been brought back within the purview of the Panchayat Union.[45]

For implementing Rural Development Programmes and other works like Minor Irrigation and Rural Dispensaries, Panchayat Unions get grant from the state government. These have to be supplemented by their own taxation efforts and by collection of public contribution for rural development programmes.[46]

Under the Tamil Nadu Panchayat Act, the sources of finance for Village Panchayats are House Tax, Profession Tax, Vehicle Tax, levy of fees on market and cart stands, licence fee on dangerous and offensive trades and duty on transfers of property and proportionate share of the proceeds of Entertainment tax. Further, on every rupee of House tax collected by a Village Panchayat, an equal amount is paid by the state government as grant which is called the village Housing Tax matching grant. A portion of local cess collected under section 115 of the Act is also paid to the Panchayat.

There are two ways the Panchayat Unions derive their income from : the revenue assigned by the state government resources raised by their efforts and the grant paid by the government for developmental schemes. They get their finance through local cess from land revenue, local cess surcharge, local cess matching grant, thirty per cent of entertainment tax from government for maintenance of roads, Minor Irrigation and Rural Dispensaries. They also get grants for development purposes like village works, social education, women and child-welfare programmes.

The elections to these bodies have not been conducted regularly since their inception. The Panchayat elections were conducted for the first time in 1965 after preparation of electoral roles covering all the Village Panchayats and Panchayat Unions. The subsequent Panchayat elections were conducted in 1970-71.

After that it was only in 1986 the elections were held with a gap of 16 years. At present, these bodies have been superseded and placed under the control of Special Officers.

Co-operatives

In the Pudukkottai state, Co-operative societies were established by introducing the British India Act of 1904 as Regulation III of 1908. In 1908 two Co-operative societies were established and this figure rose to 134 in 1944. Subsequently the British India Act of II of 1912 and Madras Co-perative Societies Act of 1935 were introduced in the state. After independence The Tamil Nadu Co-operative Societies Act of 1963 was enacted and relevant rules were framed under the Tamil Nadu Co-operative Societies Rules in 1963.[47]

The co-operative societies formed under the Act of 1961 are classified as follows : credit society, productive society, processing society, and so on. Each society has its own by-laws. However, the by-laws of these societies should be within the framework of the Act of 1961 and the Co-operative Societies Rules of 1963. All these societies in their own subject are federal in nature : a) An Apex society at the top level whose area of operation extends to the whole of the state, b) Central society at the middle level whose area of operation is confined to a part of the state and c) primary society at lower level whose area of operation is restricted to the level of the village.[48]

At the primary level the members of the society elect a managing committee among themselves to conduct the affairs of the society. The Committee members in turn elect among themselves President, Vice-President, Treasurer and Secretary. The Presidents of some of the primary societies constitute the quorum along with the nominees of government for the Central Society at the district level. The delegates of the Central Society select Board of Management and in turn the Board members select among themselves President and other office bearers. The Presidents of the Central Societies constitute the quorum along with the nominees of government for the Apex society at the state level and they in turn elect among themselves Board of Management and the Board members in turn elect among themselves President and other office bearers.

The powers and functions of Presidents and other office bearers are given in the Act of 1961, Rules of 1963 and in the by-laws of each society. The powers and functions of the Office bearers vary depends upon the nature of society.

Elections to these bodies are, like for Panchayati Raj bodies, have not been held regularly. In 1990 elections to Milk Co-operative Societies and Sheep Breeders Co-operative Societies were held. However these bodies were dissolved when AIADMK came to power in 1991 and were placed under Special Officers.

V

PERFORMANCE OF POLITICAL PARTIES IN THE ASSEMBLY ELECTIONS

To understand the role of political parties at local level, it is necessary to assess the performance of various parties at the district level in terms of number of seats won by each of them. This would show which party registered significant presence at various points of time. This would also facilitate in identifying whether the trend in the district is in confirmation with the state level.

The electoral fortunes of major political parties since 1952 in terms of number of seats won and percentage of votes polled are given in the table 2.9. The data is also given in line graphic form (graph 2.2) subsequently for better appreciation.[49]

At the state level, Congress was in power till 1967 and the DMK, between 1967 and 1975. Since 1977 till 1989 it was AIADMK, led by M.G.Ramachandran subsequently by his wife Janaki Ramachandran was in power. DMK captured power again in the State in 1989. In 1991 it was dismissed by the Chandrasekar Government at the centre. In the elections conducted to state legislature in May-June 1991 the AIADMK led by J. Jayalalitha in alliance with Congress had a sweeping majority leaving only one seat for DMK President Karunanidhi. While the state level indicates this trend what about the trend in the district ? The table 2.10 highlights the trend in the district.

From the table 2.10 it is clear that the Pudukkottai District reflects by and large state level trend in electing more number of candidates from whichever party captured power at the state level.

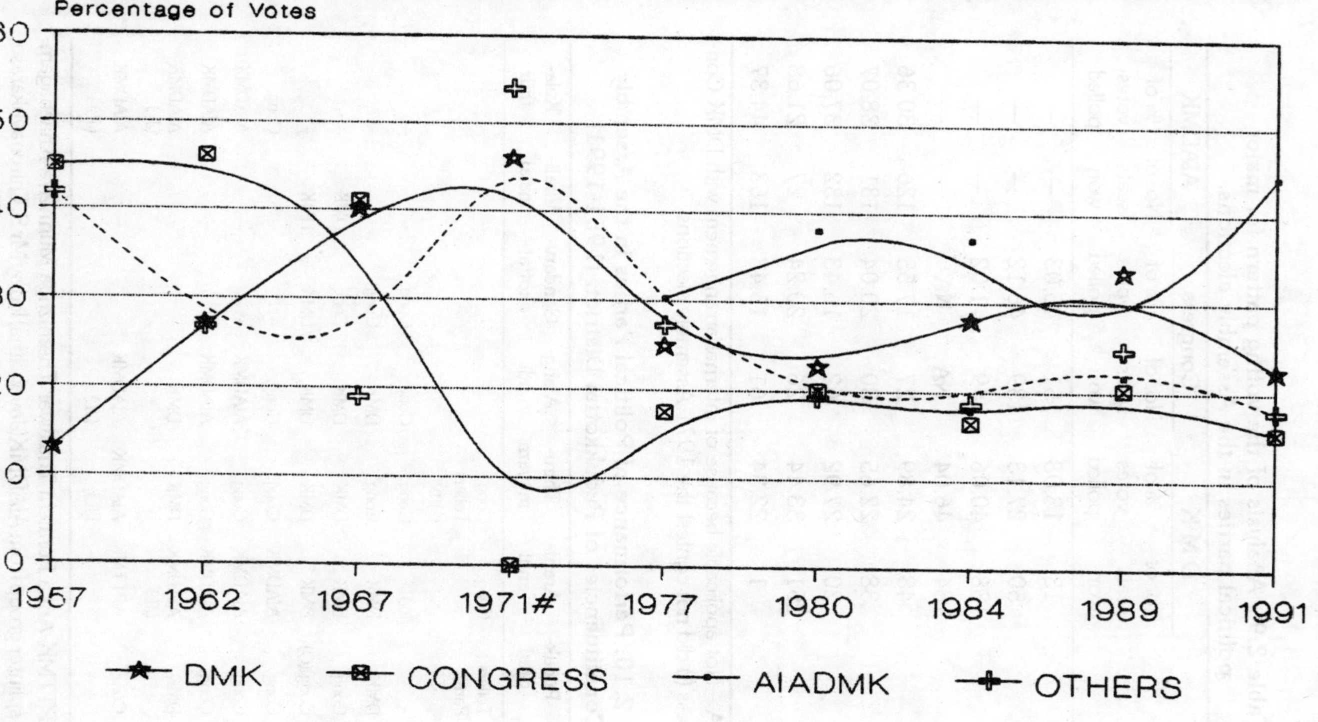

Graph 2.2 : Assembly Elections in Tamil Nadu—Performance of Political Parties

Table 2.9 : Analysis of the voting pattern for major political parties in the Assembly elections.

Year	D M K		Congress		AIADMK	
	No. of seats won	% of votes polled	No. of seats won	% of votes polled	No. of seats won	% of votes polled
1957	13	13.08	151	45.03	—	—
1962	50	27.13	139	46.12	—	—
1967	138	40.06	49	41.02	—	—
1971	184	46.04	NA	NA	—	—
1977	48	24.89	27	17.53	126	30.36
1980	38	22.65	30	20.04	131	38.07
1984	20	27.92	62	16.43	132	37.06
1989	151	33.44	26	20.24	27	21.68
1991	1	22.34	61	15.43	163	44.37

Note:- NA—Not applicable because of internal arrangement with DMK Congress (I) did not contest the 1971 Assembly elections.

Table 2.10: Performance of Political Parties in the Assembly Constituencies of Pudukkottai District. (1951-1991)

Year	Pudukottai	Arantangi	Thirumayam	Alangudi	Gandarvakottai	Viralimalai	Kulathur
1952	Toilers Party	Cong.	Cong. Toilers Party	–	–	–	–
1957	–	Ind.	Cong.	Cong.	Cong.	–	–
1962	DMK	DMK	Cong.	DMK	Cong.	–	–
1967	Cong.	DMK	DMK	DMK	Cong.	DMK	–
1971	Cong.(O)	DMK	DMK	DMK	DMK	DMK	–
1977	Cong.	AIADMK	Cong.	Cong.	–	–	Cong.
1980	Cong.	AIADMK	Cong.	AIADMK	–	–	AIADMK
1984	Cong.	AIADMK	Cong.	AIADMK	–	–	AIADMK
1989	DMK	AIADMK (JL)	DMK	DMK	–	–	AIADMK (JL)
1991	Cong.	APTTMK	AIADMK (JL)	AIADMK (JL)	–	–	AIADMK (JL)

Note : APTTMK-Anna Puratchi Thalaivar Thamizhga Munnerra Khazhagam-A splinter group from AIADMK(Jayalalitha) led by Mr S.Thirunavukarasu, then Minister in MGR cabinet got elected from Arantangi five times.

It is to be noted that the Kulathur Constituency since 1980 returned AIADMK (Jayalalitha) candidate not AIADMK (Janaki) candidate. In 1991 also it returned AIADMK candidate not a candidate from splinter group APTTMK. This goes to show that first AIADMK led by MGR and then by Jayalalitha has strong presence in Kulathur constituency in which the study area is located. DMK came to power again in 1989. At that time out of the five assembly constituencies of the Pudukkottai district DMK won in three of them. Even then Kulathur assembly constituency returned AIADMK (JL) candidate.

VI

SUMMING UP

The district is in a unique position for study as it had existed as a separate political entity and developed special relationship with the British government before Independence. It was ruled by Thondaiman Kings belonging to Kallar caste for nearly two centuries before its merger with the Indian Union. The district has other distinct features such as the urban and SC population of the district is lower than the state average. Its literacy rate is lower than state average.

The economy of the district is predominantly agrarian as majority of the population is engaged in agriculture and allied activities. It has the highest percentage of cultivators among the main workers and least of agricultural labourers. Its agriculture mainly depends on tank irrigation. The district is declared as an industrially backward area by the state government. The district consists of various caste groups of which Kallars and Valayars are numerically significant. Both groups are present in the study area in significant numbers.

Even before Independence, like in Madras Presidency, Pudukkottai State had the local self governing bodies. At present, the Panchayati Raj system is based on Tamil Nadu Panchayats Act of 1958 and Tamil Nadu District Development Councils Act of 1958. Both envisaged three tier structure with District Development Council-an advisory body, at the district level, Panchayat Unions at the block level and Village Panchayats at the village level. There are two points to be noted regarding the functioning of these bodies. Firstly, elections are not conducted regularly to these bodies.

Secondly, power of these bodies have varied from time to time.

In the district assembly constituencies mostly the parties who came to power in the state from time to time won maximum number of seats. The study area falls under Kulathur constituency, which has returned, since 1980 AIADMK candidates indicating its strong presence in the constituency.

To reiterate what was emphasised at the beginning of this chapter that the profile of the district is based on secondary data and is intended to present a general picture of the district. However, there are certain features such as caste groups, rural institutions and performance of political parties which are directly relevant to power formation and its dynamics. Other features like Population, Physiography and Ecology, Agriculture etc. are given to facilitate the understanding of the local milieu which is the focus of the next chapter.

NOTES AND REFERENCES

1. *Pudukkottai District Gazetteer* (Madras : Government of Tamil Nadu, 1983), p.5.
2. See for the history of the district K.R.Venkatrama Ayyar (ed.), *A Manual of the Pudukkottai State* Vol.II, Part I (Pudukkottai: Sri Brihadamba State Press, 1938) and S.Radhakrishna Aiyar, *A General History of the Pudukkottai State* (Pudukkottai : Sri Brihadamba State Press, 1940).
3. K.R.Venkatrama Ayyar(ed.), *A Manual of the Pudukkottai State* Vol.I (Pudukkottai : Sri Brihadamba State Press, 1938), pp.171-174.
4. *Pudukkottai District Gazetteer* op.cit., p.317.
5. Ibid, pp.32-33.
6. For soil classification of the district see *Pudukkottai District Gazetteer* op.cit., pp.293-297.
7. Ibid, p.298.

8. Ibid.
9. Ibid, p.302.
10. Ibid, pp.310-312.
11. Ibid, pp.313-325.
12. *Census of India* Part III,A and B, 1981, pp.14-16.
13. The 1931 figures for caste distribution were taken to get a broad idea about the present day numerical strength of various caste groups in the district. For composition and description of various castes in the district see K.R.Venkatrama Ayyar(ed.),Vol.I,(1938),op.cit., pp.101-137 and also *Pudukkottai District Gazetteer* op.cit., pp.208-224.
14. Nicholas B. Dirks, *The Hollow Crown : Ethnohistory of an Indian Kingdom* (Cambridge : Cambridge University Press, 1987), p.205. There were some exceptions to this status. For instance Gandarvakottai Kallars who live near the study area were branded as criminals before independence and seperate "Kallar Reclamation Schools" were started for them. K.R. Venkatrama Ayyar(ed.), Vol.I,(1938) op.cit., pp.441-442.
15. For details of different Kallar 'Nadus' and their titles see K.R.Venkatrama Ayyar(ed.), Vol.I, (1938), op.cit., pp.106-112 and for social and political structure of Kallar society particularly that of Veesinga Nadu and Ambu Nadu Kallars before independence see Nicholas B. Dirks, op.cit., pp.214-246 and 249-256.
16. *Pudukkottai District Gazetteer* op.cit., p.213.
17. Ibid, p.209.
18. Edgar B. Thurston, *Castes and Tribes of South India* Vol.V (Delhi : Cosmos, 1975), pp.206-213.
19. Ibid, p.207.
20. K.R.Venkatrama Ayyar(ed.), (1938), Vol.I, op.cit., p.124.
21. The data on the caste associations were collected during the course of fieldwork.
22. K.R.Venkatrama Ayyar(ed.), Vol.I, (1938), op.cit., p.106 and also Edgar B. Thurston, Vol.VII, op.cit., pp.272-280.
23. Edgar B.Thurston, Vol.VII, op.cit., pp.272-280.

24. Nicholas B.Dirks, op.cit., pp.270-273.
25. Ibid.
26. *Pudukkottai District Gazetteer* op.cit., p.752.
27. They are present in most of the Panchayats as evident from Census figures for 1981. *Census of India* 1981.
28. K.R.Venkarama Ayyar(ed.) Vol.I, (1938), op.cit., pp.112-115 and Edgar B. Thurston, Vol. V and VI, op.cit., pp.472-486 and 77-119 respectively.
29. K.R.Venkatrama Ayyar(ed.), Vol.I, (1938), op.cit., pp.123-124.
30. Edgar B. Thurston,Vol.II, pp.352-366.
31. K.R.Venkatrama Ayyar(ed.), Vol.I, (1938), op.cit., pp.128-129.
32. See for the list of Backward classes *Tamil Nadu Public Service Commission Bulletin* (Madras : Government of Tamil Nadu, 1989).
33. K.R.Venkatrama Ayyar(ed.),Vol.I, (1938), op.cit., pp.102-105 and 118-123 and *Pudukkottai District Gazetteer* op.cit., pp.219-224.
34. *Census of India* 1931 and 1991.
35. For the history of the local self-government in the district see *Pudukkottai District Gazetteer* op.cit., pp.653-666.
36. Ibid, p.663.
37. Ibid.
38. *The Tamil Nadu Panchayats Act of 1958* (Madras : Government of Tamil Nadu, 1959) and *District Development Councils Act of 1958* (Madras : Government of Tamil Nadu, 1959).
39. *Pudukkottai District Gazetteer* op.cit., pp.668-671.
40. G.O.MS.No.790., dated 21-10-1985, Rural Development Department, Government of Tamil Nadu.
41. S.Subramanian,"Tamil Nadu" in G.Ram Reddy, *Patterns of Panchayati Raj in India* (Delhi : Macmillan, 1977), pp.263-267.
42. Kathleen Gough, *Rural Society in South-east India* (Cam-

bridge : Cambridge University Press, 1981), p.316.

43. G.O.MS.Order No 13, dated 8-1-1986, Rural Development Department, Government of Tamil Nadu.

44. *The Tamil Nadu Panchayats Act of 1958* op.cit.

45. *The Hindu* (Madras) August 12, 1987.

46. For financial aspects of Panchayati Raj Bodies see *The Tamil Nadu Panchayats Act of 1958* op.cit.

47. Pudukkottai District Gazetteer op.cit., pp.623-623.

48. *The Tamil Nadu Co-operatives Societies Act, 1961* (Madras: Government of Tamil Nadu, 1980) and *The Tamil Nadu Co-operatives Societies Rules, 1963* (Madras : Government of Tamil Nadu, 1980).

49. V.B.Singh and Shankar Bose, *State Elections in India: Data Handbook on Vidhan Sabha Elections, 1952-85* Vol.5 (New Delhi : Sage, 1988), pp.440-609. and Pudukkottai District Gazetteer, op.cit., pp. 760-777.

The Village and its People : Towards Understanding the Milieu

This chapter discusses the salient features of the Panchayat village and its people which are relevant for the study. This chapter projects and the local milieu which provides the context for power formation and its transformation in the study village. For this purpose, different aspects covered include: location, ecology, agriculture and irrigation, settlement pattern, population characteristics, caste and religious groups, landholding, institutions and party politics. Some of these are directly or indirectly relevant. While directly relevant feature give us details about the different sources of power and power holders which are analysed in the subsequent chapters. The indirectly relevant features provide the setting for power formation and its transformation.

The location and ecology shows the position of the study Panchayat in terms of communication facilities like roads, buses etc., its proximity to urban centres, interaction among different settlements of the Udayallipatti Panchayat and ecological characteristics of the area.

Details on agriculture and irrigation covers soil classification, different seasons of cultivation, cropping pattern, extent of cultivation, rainfall situation, irrigation potential, labour activities and so on.

The population characteristics include number of males and females and occupational pattern. The settlement pattern of the Panchayat is discussed to show the caste division as reflected in the physical structure of the village. The caste and religious groups are also discussed to show the details of composition of different caste and religious groups, the ranking of different castes at the local level and religious activities of the various caste and religious groups. The landholding pattern is described to give the picture of caste and landholding pattern and land distribution.

The institutions with elected component like statutory village Panchayats and various Co-operatives like Primary Agriculture Credit Society. Milk Co-operative Society and Sheep Breeders Co-operative Society are also discussed as they are also sources of power and they also provide external linkage with outside world. Another external linkage is that of party politics which includes mobilisation of votes and political awareness.

1) LOCATION AND ECOLOGY OF THE PANCHAYAT

The Udayallipatti Panchayat consists of six settlement viz., the main village. Udayallipatti a multi-caste village with castes such as Kallars, Udayars, Konars, Pusaris, Paraiyars, etc., Chinnauranipatti-exclusively inahibited by Udayars. Alwanpatti inhabited by Kallars, Konars, Paraiyars etc., Sathrapatti consisting of Gounders and Mazavarayanvayal and Annanagar with only Pusaris living in them (See Map. II)

These settlements are not remote ones and are well connected will roads to nearest town like Pudukkottai, Thiruchirrapalli and Thanjavur and are served well with buses from early in the morning to late in the evening. These settlements are located 30 kms away from the district headquarters - Pudukkottai, and are nearest to the Block headquarters-Kunnodorkoil. In fact, the hamlet Sathrapatti, though comes under Udayallipatti Panchayat, is geographically a part of Kunnodorkoil.

At the outset, it must be mentioned that the units of this cluster inter-linked and interdependent, and in some aspects they

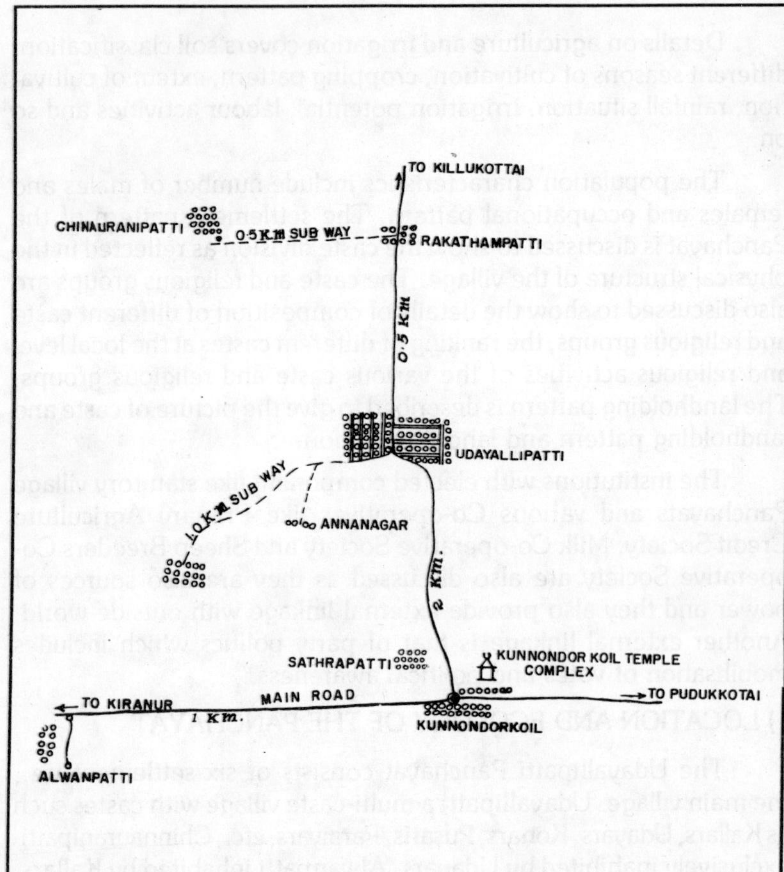

VILLAGE CASTE COMPOSITION	HAMLETS CASTE COMPOSITION
UDAYALLIPATTI : (Main Village) Kallars, Udayars, Konars, Pusaris, SCs, Asaris, Vannans, Navithars Etc.	ALWANPATTI : Kallars, Konars, Asaris, S.Cs, Etc., CHINNAURANIPATTI : Udayars only SATHRAPATTI : Gounders only MAZAVARAYANVAYAL : Pusaris only ANNANAGAR : Pusaris only

Map II : Location and Caste Composition of Udayallipatti Panchayat

are independent and have exclusiveness of their own. For instance, they are inter-linked in matters like statutory panchayat. This cluster is also treated as a single revenue unit. Thus the territorial demarcation of this cluster appears to be more out of official classification than out of general social interaction of people living in it. For example, Kinshipi network of various castes does not necessarily restrict itself to this boundary but goes beyond. They have their own boundaries.

To dwell on this point further. It is observed that physically the hamlets clustered around the main village have varying distances from the latter. The halmet Alwanpatti is approximately three and a half kms by road from the main village while the hamlets of Mazavarayanvayal, Annanagar, Chinnauranipatti are just half a km away. Sathrappati is two kms away from the main village with Gounder caste inhabiting it exclusively (See Map. II). They have no interaction with other settlements within the Panchayat in terms of kinship network. It may be that even day to day interaction of the main village is more with Rakkathanpatti, an adjacent multi-caste village because of geographical location than with Alwanpatti which is far away from the main village.

Thus, the study while taking into account these dynamics, focuses primarily on the main village in all its aspects which are relevant in the context and on its constituent units in whichever domain they are interacting with the main village.

Though at a macro-level the terrain of the area looks flat at a micro-level it has gentle slopes, uplands and low lands. These differences in the level of terrain has made it possible to construct series of tanks across the slopes to catch and exploit rain water. Generally the settlements of the area are clustered in the upper or in the middle side of the slopes. These area was supposed to have been once covered with trees are denuded. Now, the Panchayat has lands around 46 hectares classified as forest lands where social forestry department is growing mainly Eucalyptus trees.

2) AGRICULTURE AND IRRIGATION

Agriculture and its allied activities dominate the economy of the village. Most of the population is engaged in agriculture and its related activities. The following are the broad features of the agriculture and irrigation activities of the village.

There are broadly two types of soils found in the village i.e. black and red soils. Black soil is mostly found in command areas of the tanks and red soil is distributed above these tanks.

As mentioned in the previous chapter, there are broadly two seasons (Bhogam) for cultivation of various crops in a year 'Kodai' velamai and 'Kala' velamai. The latter is more extensive in terms of acreage than the former. The extent of rainfall generally decides the area of cultivation. This situation is true as far as the study village is concerned. Whenever rainfall was scanty during the last five years it has forced farmers to reduce the acreage under cultivation.

The following data for the year 1989-90 shows that under first season cultivation is more extensive than in the second seasons.[1]

It is also clear from the Table 3.1 that the dry crops like groundnut and varagu-traditional cereal grown in Tamil Nadu-occupies major portion of the cropped area. It is not only the dry crops which dominate the village agriculture but also the dry land which constitute a major area under cultivation. In the year 1989-90, 42 hectares were cultivated as wet lands and 449.519 hectares as dry lands. Under land classification, around 195 hectares come under wet land and around 975 hectares are classified as dry lands, hence, reflecting the predominance of dry land agriculture.

Table 3.1 : Extent of Cultivation under two seasons and under different crops in the Panchayat in 1989–90

Crop	First Crop		Second Crop	
	Area under Cultivation	*% of Cropped area*	*Area under Cultivation*	*% of Cropped area*
Paddy	48.770	9.60	35.920	79.12
Ground-nut	199.910	39.31	—	—
Varagu	193.945	38.19	—	—
Red gram	32.680	6.44	4.200	9.25
Sugarcane	3.980	0.78	3.980	8.77
Trees & Fruit gardens	28.520	5.62	1.300	2.86
	507.805	100.00	45.400	100.00

The dependence on dry crops is the result of a scanty rainfall as well as cultivation primarily depends on tank irrigation apart from the topography of the area. Many respondents have complained that shortage of water for irrigation has become acute during this decade and all the more during the past four or five years. To cope us with the situation, farmers with resources have resorted to digging or deepening of wells. There seems to be race for exploiting the ground water by deepening the wells each year in the face of falling water table. The reason could be that while demand for water has increased the rainfall has become scarce.

As far as tanks in the village are concerned the situation has been precarious, as common with wider area of Kalthur Taluk. Most of the tanks need two or three fills to harvest one crop of three to four months duration. The Panchayat has 22 tanks with 195 hectares under their ayacuts. The average ayacut area per tank comes to approximately nine hectares which is less than the average Kulathur taluk ayacut average area per tank, which is 11.13 hectares. Hence, it has become essential that rainfall should not only be sufficient in each season but also to be evenly spread across the season for cultivating one or two crops in a year.

This situation seems to be having an impact on labour supply situation. During the leans season, agricultural labourers mainly from Muthuraja and Scheduled Castes migrate to places like irrigated area in Thanjavur and Thiruchirrapalli town particularly Ordinance factory as casual labourers. Earlier Pannaiyal (Jajmani) system[2] had existed and now only a few farmers have 'pannaiyals'. There has been breakdown of Pannaiyal system over the years. Inspite of some Udayar and Kallar farmers. Willingness to employ permanent labour, according to information, it is difficult to get them.

Inspite of water shortage in general, farmers have wells with good irrigation potential to cultivate sugarcane and Banana crops. With this it is possible to see greenery around the village in pockets even during the summer season. Sugarcane is grown either making jaggery, which is made in adjacent villages in the crusher units, or for sugar factories.

For inputs like seeds, fertilizers and pesticides, farmers rely on private shops as well as government agricultural outlets. They sell their produce to merchants who visit the village and also in places like Pudukkottai and Thiruchirrapalli. Cultivators mainly rely on traditional instruments like plough etc. though a few hire tractors from outside for ploughing. None of the farmers own a tractor in the village. Most of them use either oil engines or electric motors for irrigation. Only a few still use 'Kavalai' a traditional mode of lifting water through bullocks. There are other agricultural activities like weeding, harvesting and winnowing which are still done by manual labour either by family labour or by engaging casual labourers.

There are other occupations which some persons engaged in are generally related to agriculture. For instance the main village Udyallipatti has been the centre for making bullock carts in the area. Some people are also engaged in basket making.

3) PEOPLE

in 1991 Udayallipatti panchayat had a population of 2140 persons with 1059 males and 1081 females living in 416 households. Out of the total Panchayat population 170 persons belong to SCs constituting 7.94 percent of the Panchayat population. This is nearly 9 percent below the district average and 11 percent below the state average. In the year 1991, the literates numbered 980 with a rate of 45.79 percent of the panchayat population. The table 3.2 illuminates the literacy ratio of the Panchayat village over the years.

The literacy in the year 1991 was 46 percent of the total panchayat population which is below the district average which is 49.70 percent of total population. The district average is less than the state average of 54.31 percent.[3]

General enquiries regarding educational level showed that the

Table 3.2 : Literacy level of the Panchayat Village

Year	Population			Literates			% of Total Population		
	M	F	Total	M	F	Total	M	F	Total
1961	674	642	1316	292	35	327	43	6	25
1971	819	793	1606	329	59	386	40	9	24
1981	842	891	1783	377	88	465	42	10	26
1991	1059	1081	2140	663	317	980	63	29	46

villages was lagging behind. Only a few persons had gone to cities and towns for salaried jobs. There is only one engineer, one supervisor and one peon working. A few young men had undergone training in III and had left the village for jobs. Presently a few boys are studying at graduate level. The situation of lack of higher education is true among Udayars who have better land man ratio than other castes and can afford economically to send their children to school.

There are basically two major trends which can be discerned as far as education is concerned. Firstly, families which cannot afford to send their children for higher education or even upto high school and secondly, parents who can afford economically but not in a position to send because their children have to take care of lands and cattles. Some of the young Udayar boys remarked with the researcher that they have to supplement their parents in looking after cattle and lands. This situation, according to them, has risen because pannaiyals from castes like Pusari and SCs are not available which has been the case earlier.

Further, two contradictory attitudes towards education exist in the minds of the people. On the one hand, the aspiration to get their children educated to put them in good jobs and on the other the negative attitude to education as expressed in the popular saying translated from Tamil. "Instead of getting educated and ruining oneself it is better to take care of cattles and become a man"

a) Occupational Pattern

Agriculture and its allied activities have been major source of livelihood, whether directly or indirectly for the majority of the population of the village as is the case with the population of the district. The table 3.3 based on 1991 census, outlines the occupational pattern of the population.

Table 3.3 : Occupational Pattern of Udayallipatti Panchayat (1991) (Percentage in brackets)

Total Population	*Main Workers*	*Marginal Workers*	*Non-Workers*
2140	773 (36.12)	350 (16.36)	1017 (47.52)

Source : Census of India, 1991.

The table 3.3 suggests that most of the population is engaged in agriculture either directly or indirectly. The above data can be arranged in terms of main workers by categories at the Panchayat level (see table 3.4).

Table 3.4 : Main workers by Categories in the Panchayat in 1991 (In percentage to total main workers)

	Cultivators	*Agricultural Labourers*	*Service Industry etc.*
Panchayat Village	70.51	17.46	12.03

Source : Census of India, 1991.

These figures suggest that among the main workers cultivators constitute the highest percentage showing direct dependence on land by the population. The above data is compared in the table 3.5 to the district and state level to find out the variations and similarities for all categories.

While in the Panchayat, the percentage of cultivators is higher district which in turn is higher than the state. However, the Panchayat shows lesser percentage of agriculture labour than both district and state figures.

Table 3.5 : Comparative statement of Main Workers by Categories in 1991 at the Panchayat, District and State Levels

(In percentage)

	Cultivators	*Agricultural Labourers*	*Service Industry etc.*
Panchayat	70.51	17.46	12.03
District	48.60	25.85	25.55
State	24.84	34.63	40.52

Source : Census of India, 1991.

4) SETTLEMENT PATTERN: THE MAIN VILLAGE AND ITS HAMLETS

Udayallipatti has three main streets running from east to west and small streets cutting them from north to south (see map III). The north and northwest of the main street is occupied by Udayar along with Asaris, Muslims, Pandarams etc., while to the south of it is occupied by Kalars, along with Muslims, Asaris, Konars etc. only exception being one Kallar buying a house is what is supposed to be udayar area. The physical distance between areas of other caste houses and what is now called Harijan Colony (paraicheri) is a road which divides between these settlements. However, one prominent Kallar has not only bought but is also living in a house constructed by Muslim just adjacent to Harijan Colony. There are a few families of Pusaris who are treated socially above Parayiyars but below other castes. They are settled in the north western portion of the village. Generally speaking the physical and imaginary segregation or demarcation between different caste houses is no longer rigid and clear cut as was the case earlier. The earlier exclusiveness of udayar and Kallar area is breaking down, though it is not so yet between Scheduled castes, Pusaris and the other castes.

As shows earlier the hamlet of Chinnauranipatti is exclusively inhabited by Udayrs; Sathrapatti by Gounders and Mazhavarayanvayal and Annanagar by Pusaris. Like Udayallipatti, the hamlet of Alwanpatti is a multi-caste village consisting of Kallar, Konar, Asari and Scheduled caste house. Generally all are just one or two street settlements. While hamlets like Chinnauranipatti, Mazhavarayanvayal, Annanagar are approximately half a km away across the main village, the hamlet Satharapatti is one km away and Alwanpatti is three kms away by road from the main village. It is necessary to point out both Satharapatti and Alwanpatti are not only physically at a distance from the main village but are also for general day to day interactions and other matters which will be dealt subsequently.

5) COMPOSITION OF CASTE GROUPS

The Udayallipatti Panchayat is a multi-caste and multi-religious village. As on 1988, it has approximately 379 households with 1337 votes. These households and votes distributed between the main village Udayallipatti (here afterwards called the main village) and five other constituent settlements. As noted earlier, while the main village and Alwanpatti are inhabited by many caste and religious groups and other settlements are occupied by a single caste. The following table (3.6) based on 1988 voters list shows the various castes and religious groups living in the Panchayat village. (see pie graph 3.1)

From the table 3.6 it may be discerned that Kallar constitute the largest groups of 127 households with 494 voters. After Kallars

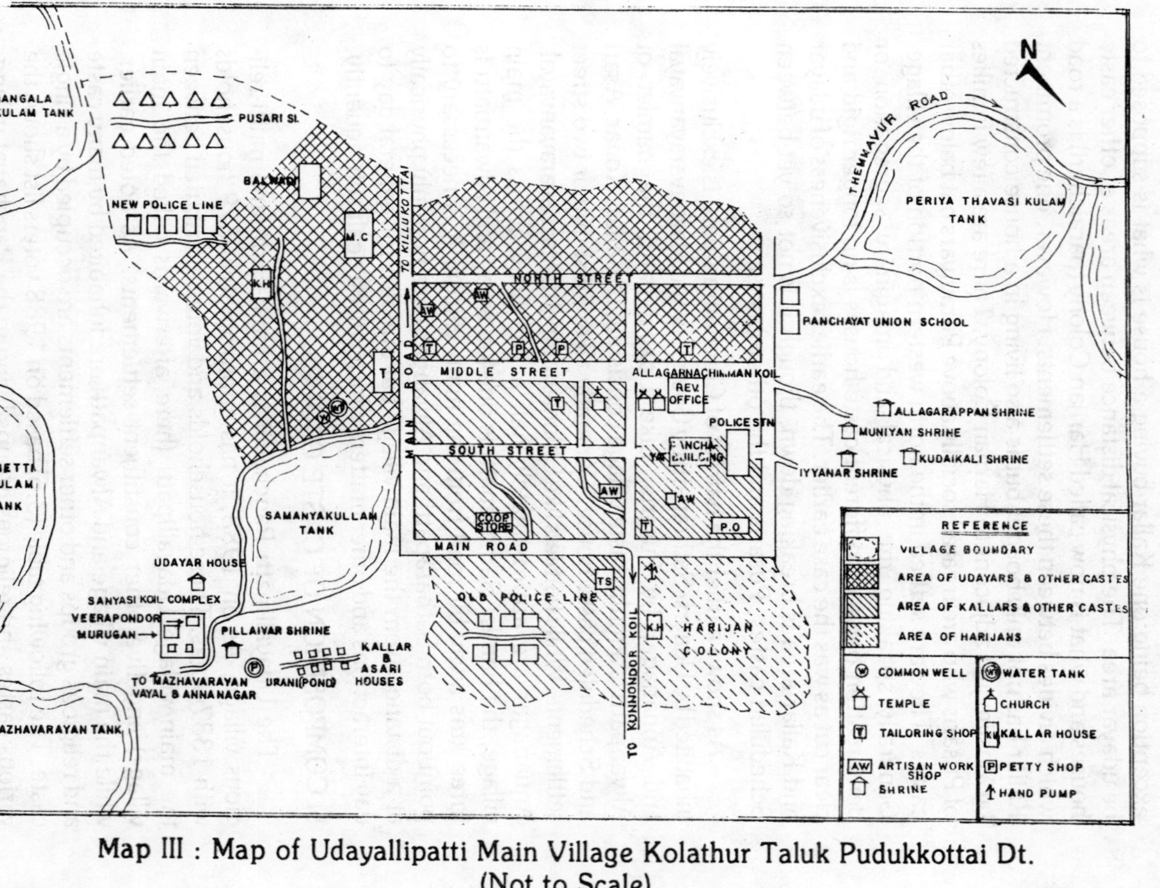

Map III : Map of Udayallipatti Main Village Kolathur Taluk Pudukkottai Dt.
(Not to Scale)

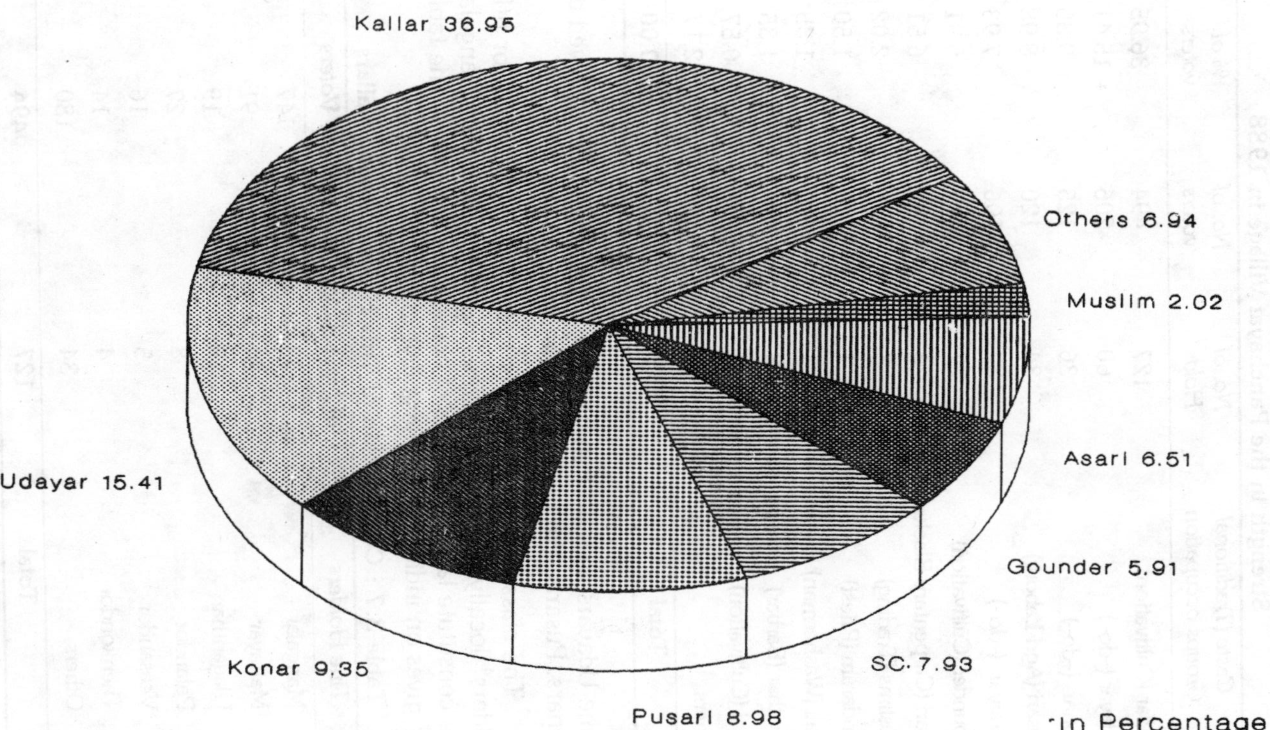

*In Percentage

Graph 3. 1 : Voting Strength of Various Castes* Udayallipatti Panchayat

Table 3.6 : Caste and Religious Groups and their Voting Strength in the Panchayat Village in 1988

Caste (Traditional Groups occupation	*No. of Holds*	*No. of voters*	*% of voters*
Kallar (Cultivation)	127	494	36.95
Udayar (–do–)	60	206	15.41
Konar (–do–)	36	125	9.35
Pusari (Agri Labour)	34	120	8.98
Paraiyar (–do–)	32	106	7.93
Gounder (Cultivation)	27	79	5.91
Asari (Carpentary Blacksmithy)	26	87	6.51
Muslims (Trading)	8	27	2.02
Pandaram (Priest)	7	20	1.50
Egali (Washerman)	5	18	1.35
Navithar (Barbar)	5	18	1.35
Pillai (Cultivation)	2	8	0.57
Others	10	29	2.17
Total	**379**	**1337**	**100.00**

come Udayars with 60 households having 206 voters followed by Konars, Pusaris, Paraiyars and other caste groups.

The classification of Kallars in terms of subdivision or title holders[4] (locally called pattaperyrs) show that Kallars with Mangalar title constitute largest number of households and votes. The table 3.7 gives on indication of these divisions among Kallars.

Table 3.7 : Composition of Title Holders among Kallars

Title Holders	*No. of Households*	*No. of Voters*
Mangalar	43	147
Mattayar	24	91
Ulaganthar	9	19
Palandor	8	27
Veesandor	5	16
Thenkondor	4	14
Others	34	180
Total	**127**	**494**

6) CASTE GROUPS AND STRUCTURE

After having dealt with the numerical strength of various caste and religious groups in the village, this section deals first with the board features of different caste groups and their inter-relationships and subsequently with the religious groups and their religious activities.

In dealing with caste groups, only those features that are relevant i.e., original place from where they have migrated, if known, kinship network and distribution of each caste in around the study area, social ranking of different caste at the village level, traditional occupation and continuity and changes in occupation, caste panchayat and tradition and role of caste associations are presented. The other features of caste groups such as religious activities of various groups and landholding of each caste groups and discussed separately.

Kallars

According to local understanding Kallars of the main village were from a nearby settlement called 'Verrimangalam' which no longer exists now. Gradually they were allowed to settle in the present village which was supposed to be earlier predominantly Udayar caste settlement. Beyond this, the Kallar informants were not sure from where they have migrated. Historically, Kallars of this area migrated many centuries before from norther Tamil Nadu.

As noted in the preceding chapter Kallars have endogamous territorial divisions called 'Nadus' which in turn is divided into many exogamous patrilineal clans. The main village belongs to broader and bigger nadu called 'Visenginadu' comprising of many smaller nadus. At a local level it belongs to Vadamlai Nadu. Generally earlier Kallars of different nadus did not intermarry but it is no longer so. Within each nadu each exogamous pratilineal clan has a distinct name as it is locally called 'pattapeyar' or title. Families within the titles do not intermarry as they considered 'pangalis' or blood relatives.

In the villages there are around twenty different title holders. Among them, as we have seen earlier, Kallar with 'Mangalar' title are in a majority both in terms of number of households and voters as well as the extent of land holding. They are believed to be original settlers or clan or a kind of 'sons of soil' in the main village. The Kallars with other titles have primarily married into the families of Mangalars. They came to be called persons belonging to 'ponnadi Kannika' or persons married to girls in the village. The Mangalar title holders are in turn divided into three Karais viz., Upper, Middle and Lower.

It is interesting to note that the Presidents of village panchayat so far have belonged to one of these Karais. Further, before 1947 village headman or 'Ambalar' was from upper Karai Mangalar family. Local people still refer to the family as Ambalar family. Ambalar was acting as an intermediary between local population and king for collection of revenue and maintaining law and order. He also acted as an adjudicator of village disputes. In other nearby villages Kallars were also given Mirasadar title performing the duty of revenue collection. However, in the main village, there are two Udaya families which were earlier conferred with Mirasadar title.

In the study area Kallars are distributed widely and according to local informants they are present, in varying numerical strength in almost all the villages in the surrounding area. The kinship network of Kallars of the main village, however, extends only to the nearby areas. For instance, Kallars of Udayallipatti have more marriage alliances with adjacent Rakkathampatti and Oduganpatti villages than far away villages. The kinship network of kallars makes it possible to seek help to settle family and caste disputes by relatives easily.

The kinship network was not only restricted to family and caste disputes but also to inter nadu and inter village panchayats. The inter village disputes were generally solved by important elders of the different villages. However, these panchayats are no longer as effective as they were, despite this some important men of different villages are adjudicating disputing involving more than one village.

With Kallars of the area, there is a tradition of 'aggressiveness' and they are known for their dominance in behaviour.[5] They evoke fear in the minds of other caste people with a threat to use violence. Though difficult to generalize this characteristics to all Kallars, informants from both Kallar and other castes by and large confirmed this point. It is found that during the period of field work, it was the Kallars who were in the lead in all village matters whether of temple festivals or settlement of inter-caste disputes.

Earlier, as noted in the previous chapter, Kallars were making a living by 'Thuppukuli' system. This was true in the study area too. The elderly respondents still recollected with pride the daring exploits of lifting cattles and house robbery by their ancestors. Some of the Kallars involved in these exploits have become legendary figures. However, the early ways of living have disappeared over the years because of institutions of police, judiciary, etc. Kallars have now turned into settled agriculturists. In the village, they are now mostly cultivators and with education some of them have taken up jobs outside the village.

As it was mentioned earlier, Kallars are part of Mukkulathor Association. Though generally respondents were aware of its existence and a few had attended a meeting organised at district level in mid 80s, none of them, however, was an active-members of the association or has made any efforts to enlist as a member of the association.

Udayars

Next to Kallars, Udayars is the populous caste with 59 households and 206 voters. The Udayars are represented both in the main village and in another settlement called Chinnauranipatti. In fact, it is exclusively inhabited by nearly twenty Udayar families. They have day to day interaction as well as marriage alliance etc., with the Udayars of the main village. They divided into southern and northern sections, and upper and lower divisions in the main village.

The Udayars were supposed to have migrated from places like Perambulur and Udayarpalaym, Anjanur and Vallam in Thiruchirrapalli and Thanjavur districts to Kulathur taluk of the Pudukkottai district. Each Udayar family is identified with a place of family deity or 'Kanikoil'. Same Kanikoil people do not intermarry. According to local informants their kinship network beyond the taluk boundaries. The Udayars of the village belong to 'Nathaman' division. The Christian Udayars are present in pockets of Kunnondorkoil Panchayat Union. The Hindu and Christian Udayars however do not intermarry.

Like in the wider areas of the Pudukkottai district the Udayars of the village do not have any caste panchayat of their own. In case of disputes either within or outside the caste, Udayar would approach Kallars or go to court for settlement.

While describing the caste traditions of the Udayars even informants from other castes concede that Udayars are hard working, thrift minded and frugal in their ways of living. They are called 'Boomi Palagans' i.e. Sons of Earth. Most of the Udayars are still following their age younger generation have gone out to towns and cities in search of modern occupations.

The Udayars have caste association called Parkavakula Sangam which includes Nathaman, Surithimmar, Malayaman, Moopanar and Nainar. In 1985 the Sangam organised a meeting which was attended by political party leaders, including some ministers from the AIADMK Government and Congress leader G.K. Moopanar, irrespective of party affiliations. Some Udayars from the village had also attended the meeting in which the speakers mainly dealt on the education of Parkavakula youths so as to equip them to compete for various modern jobs. Subsequently neither membership drive nor any other activity by the association was reported by the respondents in the village.

Konars

The Konars are otherwise known as Idaiyars. They are generally shepherds by profession. There are a few families of Konars who live in the main village and round 30 families live in Alwanpatti sharing the settlement with Kallars predominantly having 'mattayar' title.

The Konars do not have strong caste panchayat system as Kallars. However, in case of disputes they try to settle them among themselves. Where it is not possible they approach Kallars particularly from Udayallipatti for settlement.

Though traditionally the occupation of Konars was cattle rearing over the years they have acquired lands and since then cultivation has become an occupation more important than cattle breeding.

Pusaris

The Valayars, as noted in the earlier chapter, are locally called Pusaris. Officially they are called Mutharajas. Generally people in the locality address them as Pusaris. The settlements of Pusaris are scattered with a few houses in the main village, and in other two settlements namely Mazhavarayanvayal and Annanagar. The ancestors of Pusaris were supposed to have migrated from nearby areas. The marriage alliances are decided not on the basis of family deities but on the basis of familiarity of kinship network. As Dirks mentions they are wide-spread in the district.[6] The Pusaris do not have caste panchayat of their own like Kallars. Largely they try to settle small disputes within the caste by the elders of the caste. However, in general, they approach Kallars from the main village for adjudication of disputes within and with other castes. Traditionally the occupation of Pusaris was netting game in jungle. Now mostly they work as casual labourers for digging wells in the area and some are cultivators. Of late, many people, particularly men, go to ordinance factory at Thiruchirrapalli to work as industrial casual labour.

The Pusaris also have an association called Muthurajas Association. None of the local Pusaris it appears is an active member though they are members of the Association. Some caste people from the village attended the Association meeting which took place not long ago in Thiruchirrapalli. Earlier they were engaged in the works like digging graves, making tents (Pandal) for marriages. Now, they have stopped doing them at the instance of their Association.

Paraiyars (SC)

The Paraiyars and Pallars are scheduled castes of the area. However, only Paraiyars are living in the village particularly in the main village and two families are living in Alwanpatti settlement. Earlier there was a clear cut physical exclusion of the SC settlements from the main village. Now, only a road divides the main villages and what is now called, Harijan Colony. Infact, a prominent Kallar bought a house constructed by a Muslim which is part of the Colony and is living there. They are widely spread in Kulthur taluk and they are settled in all the Panchayat villages.[7] Interestingly, a person from SC whose family was the earliest to settle in the village, is a priest of some of the shrines in the village.

Like Kallars, Paraiyars also have a tradition of caste panchayats. Generally disputes arising within the caste are settled by caste elders. If matter is not settled within caste they would approach

Kallars for the purpose.

Tradionally, Paraiyars were mainly agricultural labours and mostly worked as 'Pannaiyals' for Udayrs and Kallars. Now that the Pannaiyal system has practically disappeared. Now they mostly work as casual labourers during the peak seasons in the village and in the lean seasons migrate to Cauvery delta, situated beyond the northern boundary of the district. Apart from this few young caste men are educated and have taken up jobs. One of them is an engineer and is the only engineer from the village.

Gounders

In the beginning of the chapter it was mentioned that Gounders exclusively habitating Satharapatti settlement have interaction with the main village as an officially demarcated unit as part of Village Panchayat and revenue unit. Apart from these two domains of interaction for disputes arising within castes generally they approach the Kallars from the main village for settlement. Most of them are cultivators holding lands under tanks which are exclusively occupied by the caste.

Asaris

The Panchayat Village has both Christian and Hindu Asaris. Like a few other castes, Hindu Asaris also have places of family deity which determines marriage alliances. Though locally they are called Asaris they come under the category of Kammalar Caste. The Hindu Asaris belong to Vishwakarma section.

Both Hindu and Christian Asaris are servicing castes. Tradionally they were assigned five occupations, as mentioned earlier. In the village there are now only Thachans (Carpenters) and Kollans (Blacksmith). As of now some of them have migrated to urban areas while others have given up the earlier profession of Goldsmith to take up other traditional occupations of the caste. A few young men have taken up jobs as electricians and the like. Some of the caste men own lands and cultivate them. The main village has been the centre for making bullock-carts and continues to be one though with less demand for it than earlier. Earlier they were paid either in kind or cash, however, now only cash is being paid for their work.

Both Hindu and Christian Asaris belonged to an association called Vishwakarma Association. A few years back two Asari young men visited the village seeking membership drive and urging them to unite so as to bargain for better wages. A few, it was reported, did enrol as member. It seems there has not been any follow-up on this by the Association.

OTHER CASTE GROUPS

There are other servicing castes like Navithar (Barbers) Egali (Washermen) are still pursuing their traditional occupation apart from owning and cultivating lands. Earlier for their servicing they were paid in kind and cash now only cash is being paid.

The persons belonging to Pandaram caste are temple priests for the middle castes like Kallars, Udayars etc. Apart from the traditional priestly occupation they also own lands. There is no Brahmin family left in the village now. However, till recently there was one Brahmin in the village who was the Karnam or village accountant. Some Brahmin families earlier owned lands under this Panchayat area though no longer residents of the village. Further, Brahmins from adjacent Kunnondorkoil owned lands falling under Udayallipatti Panchayat earlier.

The trading casting like Chettiars were once residents and owned lands extensively in the village. None of them is living in the village now and only their descendants still visit the village to take care of whatever lands left after selling their ancestral properties including houses. The Muslim households and a Pillai household are owning petty shops in the main village and they also own lands.

The above mentioned caste groups can be arranged hierarchically on the basis of local ranking as shown in the Table 3.8

The table 3.8 shows that Kallars, Udayars, Konars and Gounders also situated in the upper position of the local hierarchy and most of them are cultivators. In the middle, servicing caste like Asari, Pandaram, Egali and Navithar are placed and apart from

Table 3.8 : Local ranking of different castes in the Panchayat village

Social Position	*Caste*
Upper	Udayar, Kallari, Konar, Gounder
Middle	Asari, Pandaram, Egalir, Navithar
Lower	Pusari, SC

serving their castes also some of them own lands. The lowest in the local hierarchy are Pusaris and Paraiyars (SC). However, compared to SCs, Pusaris are treated socially higher. Both the castes were earlier serving upper castes like Udayars and Kallars as Pannaiyals now they work as casual labourers. Though many of the castes have their caste associations none of the persons from these caste are active in their respective association activities.

7) RELIGIOUS GROUPS AND THEIR ACTIVITIES

The Hindus constitute the majority of the village population, Christians and Muslims are fewer in number. The Christians of the village are from Asari caste and they still follow their traditional occupations. Despite change in the religious faith, some of them still wear thread across the chest like Brahmins at least during Avani Avitam. They now belong to Roman Catholic division. There is a church constructed recently in the centre of the village for them. The Muslims also have a place of worship situated in the fields outside the residential area.

For Hindus, temples and shrines are located in the residential area of the village and beyond but within village boundaries. One of them is Sri Veerapondor Temple which is situated half a km away in the south-west of the main village and is as much as 100 years old. Some temples like Priddari and Kaliamman Koils are new ones constructed from temple funds and public donations (see Map. III).

Of all the temples and shrines Sri Veerapondor temple has been the major centre of religious activities of the village. It is also known as Sannayasi Koil. Within temple complex there are four deities that is apart from the principal deity, Sri Veerapondor, Murugan-son of Shive and Parvathi, Madurai Veeran and Karuppannaswamy. Just in front of this complex Vinayagar is situated at the edge of a drinking water pond called 'urani'. Veerapondor temple has trustee appointed by the government to run the affairs of the temple and it has around 52 acres of land which was given to Mangalars as grant by the Pudukkottai kings for its maintenance and to conduct festivals.[8] Apart from this income, contributions from the public are also mobilised for priest for conducting daily pujas. The important festivals in the temple complex are Vijaya Dasami, Panguni Uthiram, Sivarathri, and Karthigai Theepam. For the last five or six years the festivals of the temple could not be conducted regularly because of dispute between two factions of Kallars.[9] In these festivals 'Prasadam' is given first to Ambalar belonging to Kallar caste in the main village there by giving the status of first person in the village.[10]

Two other temples which are located in the centre of the main village are Piddari Amman or Nachhiamman and Kalliamman temples. These temples also have Pandaram as the priest and these temples are maintained by public contributions and income from lands belonging to them. First prasadam in these temples is not given to Ambalar but to government officials or to outsiders. In Veerapondor and in the two other temples harijans are not allowed to enter but they participate from outside.

There is a cluster of four shrines lying in the eastern of the main village. Interestingly a SC person is the priest for all these shrines. In these shrines SCs also offer prayer along with people from other castes. This cluster include Alaggappan deity of Kallars, Kudai Kalli, Ayyenar and Munian. Though Alaggapan is a Kallar deity Udayars also visit and offer brass bells to be fixed in the temple for the deity having heard and fulfilled their prayers. Apart from these temples and shrines there are innumerable others spread over entire village boundaries as family deities or deities to protect against diseases. One of them is Kalliamman shrine constructed in 1990 by a SC leader with financial help from his fellow caste men, political leaders, government officials etc.

Along with these religious activities another trend is discernible during the recent years i.e., visiting temples of Murugan at Palani and Ayyappan at Sabarimalai, Kerala.[11] Though a few people in the main village have started visiting these temples in the early eighties more recently thirty to forty people visit each year and some of them more than once after fasting and doing other rituals for a specific number of days. It is important to note that it is not only upper level castes like Kallars, Udayars who visit these temples, but also SCs and Pusaris particularly to Ayyappan temple. One of the persons from SC visited temple three times in recent years.

Enquiries with people who have visited as to why they have visited such far away place as a part of the religious activity evoked varied responses from different people. Some of them said that it is an individual faith and others commented that the very hardship involved in fasting and reaching the temples by walk appeals to them. One youth explained that during fasting days Ayyappan temple devotees have to call each other respectably as 'swamy' irrespective of caste, class and age. He believed that this temporary situation of mutual respect holds on even after returning from the temple.

8) CASTE AND LANDHOLDING

The Udayallipatti Panchayat is a revenue unit including the main village Udayallipatti and its hamlets i.e. Chinnauranipatti, Mazhavarayanvayal, Annanagar, Sathrapatti and Alwanpatti. Mostly people belonging to the Panchayat own lands in its jurisdiction. However, people from other villages or Panchayats or residents who have now left to towns and cities also own lands in the revenue area, though fewer in number compared to present residents. Further, even the residents may own lands in other Panchayats. To put it is a nutshell, the aspect of caste and landholding in the study Panchayat, cannot be totally and precisely isolated and studied. Thus, with these limitations in mind an attempt is made to study the relationship between caste and their landholdings.

The study of caste and landholding is done by comparing land records of the revenue village at two points of time i.e. in 1960 and 1990, a gap of thirty years. The table 3.9 gives caste-wise landowners, their total holdings and percentage for each caste out of total lands owned in the village.[12] (see also bar graph 3.2)

Perusal of the table suggests that both Kallars and Udayars together owned 50 percent in 1960 and 58 percent in 1990 of the lands. The Udayars in 1960 have possessed 26 percent of total land and has more or less same percentage of landholding in 1990 The Kallars have increased their landholding from 24 percent in 1960 to 32 percent in 1990. In 1960 total lands of Udayars was more than that of Kallars and in 1960 it is the other way round. However, Udayars in 1990 had 4.72 acres per owner compared 2 acres among Kallars.

While the total landholding of Kallars and Udayars has increased, the landholding of Chettiars, Muslims and Brahmins has decreased over the years. This is in confirmation with the version of various informants that the latter possessed much more lands earlier say even 20 years back than now. In particular, few Chettiar families owned lands extensively before thirty to forty years.

Table 3.9 : Caste-wise Holdings of Udayallipatti Revenue Village in 1960 and 1990

No. Caste	1960			1990		
	Land Owners (No.)	Tl. lands Owned (acres)	%	Land Owners (No.)	Tl. lands Owned (acres)	%
1. Kallars	184	615.60	24	391	859.39	32
2. Udayars	132	664.08	26	148	699.01	26
3. Konars	62	231.08	9	92	302.30	11
4. Pusaris	41	102.73	4	94	199.26	8
5. Gounders	21	49.72	2	44	117.87	5
6. Asaris (H+CH)	23	34.93	1	41	67.90	3
7. Muslims	19	54.34	2	15	43.15	1
8. Chettiars	10	123.60	5	8	34.26	1
9. Brahmins	5	15.66	0.62	9	12.50	0.47
10. Pillai	4	7.48	0.29	17	18.35	0.69
11. Pandaram	2	13.59	0.53	10	21.51	0.81
12. Naicker	3	9.16	0.36	3	15.59	0.59
13. Egali	2	5.98	0.24	7	9.54	0.36
14. Naidu	Not	Known	----	3	16.56	0.59
15. S.C.	-do-	-do-	----	29	37.25	1.00
16. Others	380	615.80	24.00	155	221.16	8.38
	878	**2,544.40**	**100.00**	**1066**	**2,653.75**	**100.00**
Temple lands, etc.		1,991.26			1,071.18	
Grand Total		3,735.65			3,735.65	

Probably this prompted one respondent to say that the whole village was a Chettiar village once. Gradually the descendants of these families sold off their lands, mostly to Kallars as they were their former tenants.

An interesting feature of the 1960 land record is that lands of Kallars and Udayars broadly fell under different tanks. This situation continues even now except a few cases of Kallar lands in Udayar area. According to elderly informants this demarcation has been there for a long time.

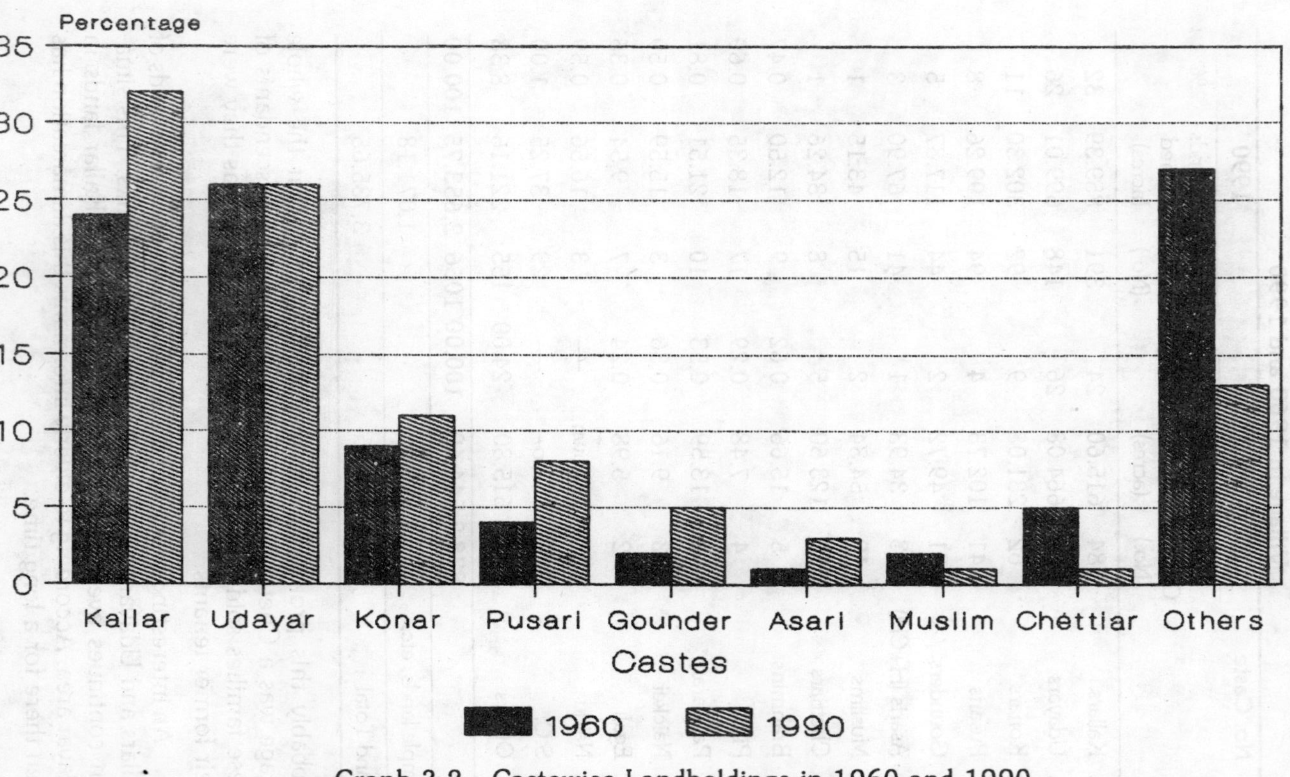

Graph 3.2 : Castewise Landholdings in 1960 and 1990
Udayallipatti Panchayat

9) LANDHOLDING CATEGORIES:

Unlike in the past when land holding was concentrated in a few now the ownership is diffused. Some landowners from Udyar, Kallar, even Pusari castes can be identified as big landowners having 20 or more acres. The table 3.10 gives the landholding pattern in 1990. The data is also presented as bar graph (3.3.) after the table.

Table 3.10 : Different Categories of Landholders in 1990

Category	*No. of land holders*	*Percentage to total landholders*	*Total Land-holding (in acres)*	*Percentage to total lands owned*
a	460	43	158.53	6
b	266	25	430.35	16
c	199	19	697.95	26
d	96	9	667.95	25
e	25	2	306.06	12
f	20	2	393.30	15
Total	**1066**	**100**	**2653.76**	**100**

The preceding table suggest that nearly 86 percent of the landowners hold less that 2.50 acres, while for the district as a whole it is around 80 percent and for the state it is 69 percent.

10) INSTITUTIONS

In the study area only those institutions which have elected body like Village Panchayat and Co-operatives and studied in detail. It is not to say other institutions like revenue, health, police which are bodies of the state governments do not have any role to play to in the village. However, passing mention has been made to get to an idea of different institutions operating in this area. Some of them are development oriented in the context of various rural development programmes and some are service oriented.

a) Village Panchayat

It was noted earlier that Village Panchayat is the basic unit of panchayat system in Tamil Nadu. The Udayallipatti panchayat consists of the main village and its four hamlets. It is part of Kunnondorkoil Panchayat union consisting of 38 Panchayats which

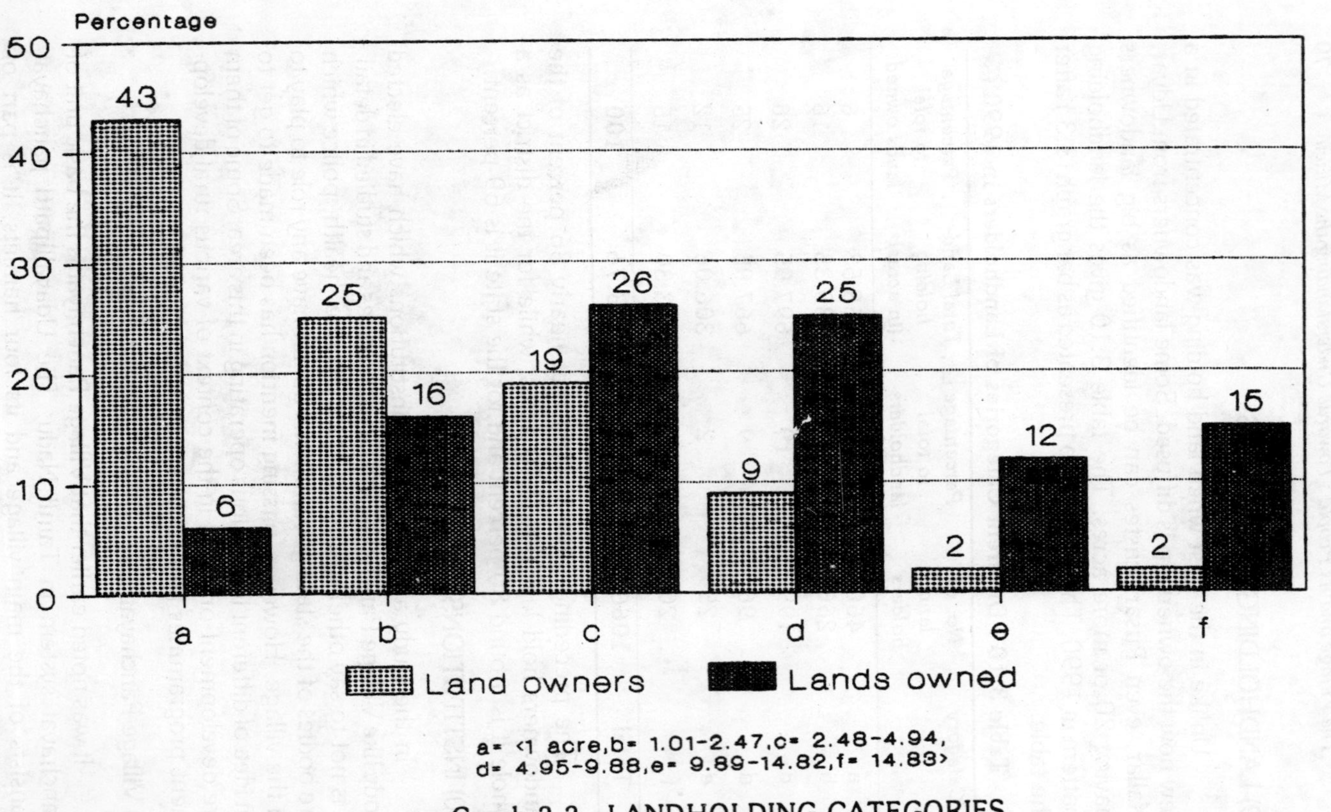

Graph 3.3 : LANDHOLDING CATEGORIES
Udayallipatti Panchayat

includes a Town Panchayat as well.

Each village Panchayat board consist of a president, a Vice President and members of different wards including two reserved wards i.e. one for women and another for SCs. The term of Village Panchayat Board is for five years.

In the Panchayat elections conducted in February 1986, for the post of President the contest was between the same traditional contenders i.e. two Kallars-HM and QM-with Mangallar title and both of them contested in the 1970 Panchayat elections well. HM has been President for three terms. It was only in 1986 QM got elected as the President. In 1986 of 990 valid votes polled while HM got 454 votes and QM got 536 votes.

The President of Village Panchayat has an important role to play in the implementation of various rural development programmes. Under various rural development schemes the Udayallipatti panchayat has acquired the following infrastructures over the years-common well and drinking water supplied through a bore well with over-head tank (a new one was under construction at the time of the study), Panchayat building with Ratio and TV facilities, maternity centre (yet to start functioning). Balwady (non meal scheme centre) and school building. Many old roads were given face lift. Some new roads are paved from time to time, bunds of tanks have been strengthened and sluices of tanks have also been renovated.

b) Co-operatives

There are co-operatives like Primary Agriculture Credit Society, Milk Co-operative Society, Sheep breeders Co-operative Society operating in the area. Some societies like Primary Agriculture Credit Society has been operating in the area for more than two decades, others are of recent developments. Each have their own boundaries or villages under their jurisdiction and operation. Like Panchayati Raj bodies, elections to the various Co-operatives have not been held regularly. During one of the field visits, there was one election taking place for the position for President of Milk Co-operative Society in which Kallar with Mattayar title won. He was earlier elected as a President to Sheep breeders Co-operatives Society.

c) Other Institutions

There are other institutions like Village Revenue Office, Primary Health Centre, Post Office, Police Stations (established as an out post nearly 70 years back) and fair price shop in the main village. There are commercial banks, land Development Bank and many government departments like Agriculture, Education, Health, Social Welfare, Social Forestry etc., operating through Panchayat union in this area. There are non-governmental organisations (NGOs) like Thiruchirrappalli Multi-purpose Service Society (TMSS) which is organising women for self employment and 'Kudumbam' an organisation working on ecological farming, are also operating in the area.

11) PARTY POLITICS

The party politics at local level is at to be studied through the pattern of vote mobilisation, political awareness of voters and party preferences of voters. Before taking up these it is to be mentioned about what are all the parties operating in the area. According to respondents earlier Congress and DMS were active in the village. After the emergence of AIADMK it registered its presence in the area. There were few cadres of CPM also present in the village.

The often repeated opinion of the various respondents is what generally people no longer vote on the basis of what elders of the village say as was common earlier but it is now more on the basis of their party affiliations or personal preferences. One elderly informant from Kunnondor Koil, during the course of the interview with him, recollected the voting behaviour of the people. Earlier, Congress party bosses along with candidate of the area would land up in Mirasidars or Ambalars houses and the whole village was called and told to vote for their candidate. Another informant reflected the trend in a similar way by saying "Earlier people voted according to what elders said and now each one, including members of the same family, has individual party preferences", It is common in the village to find different brothers having different party affiliations. For instance, in one Kallar family among four brothers one is a Congressman, another important party functionary in AIADMS, one belongs to DMK and while another belongs to Communist party. This is generally applicable to people from other castes also.

Another aspect of change in political consciousness is that of mobilisation of votes through campaign. Earlier local leaders would call important men from other castes and ask for votes. Now each party cadre or local party leaders have to visit houses, including those of Schedule Caste, to canvass for votes.[13]

Now though local leaders may be recruited for mobilization of votes the appeals of political parties directly seem to play increasing role in the electoral process. Further, local party leaders based on party affiliation seems to have emerged more influential than that of caste and panchayat leaders. It may be recognition of increased role of party politics in the villages., AIADMK government in 1986 announced that parties with their symbols could put up candidates for elections both for Panchayat Unions and Village Panchayats. However, this order was partially withdrawn allowing political party candidates for Panchayat Unions only without assigning any reason.[14]

Another feature of this trend is the contribution of mass media particularly newspapers to political awareness. Though exact impact is not clear yet certainly it contributes to discussion on political matters at local level. It is to discussion on political matters at local level. It is common to find people obviously men in tea shops not only in the study village but also in wider area discussing about politics ranging from state to national level.[15] In fact, in the main village, the day starts with men assembling in the tea shops to have tea. When the newspaper subscribed by the Village Panchayat arrive by bus around 6 o'clock some of the readers would start reading the paper loudly. Even uneducated audience would listen to the news carefully. This starts off discussion and comments on what is happening in politics and about political leaders. Some times there would be heated discussion among different party supporters on actions or pronouncement of party leaders. This goes on for sometime till many of them drift away gradually to their fields for work. Observing these discussions QM once commented to the researcher.

"I am not happy about this, I also have party preference and belong to congress party. No doubt there should be discussions about politics, but not in this way. Different party cadres and supporters abuse each other. Today different party leaders abuse each other in the public platforms or through the press but tomorrow they would join hands together according to their conveniences. In this kind of situation why should we fight among ourselves".

SUMMING-UP

This chapter, thus, has focused on relevant features of the Udayallipatti Panchayat which are necessary for the study. The description of relevant features while focusing on the main it has also taken note of interaction between the main village and its constituent units in whichever domain they have been interacting.

The main features of the Panchayat are as in the case of the district, people in the village are dependent on agriculture and its allied activities as a main source of livelihood. They also depend on rainfall and dry land agriculture. A marked feature in the occupational pattern of the panchayat population is the higher percentage of cultivators among main workers compared to the district and state figures. Other feature of the panchayat includes low level of agricultural mechanization, predominance of tank irrigation, decline of pannaiyal system and emergence of wage labour.

The statement pattern of the main village reflects the board caste hierarchy at the local level. The caste structure is marked by hierarchy of local ranking with Kallars, Udayars etc., on the upper strata, servicing casters like Asaris, Vannars etc., are in the middle and the lowest among all are Pusaris and SCs who are mainly agricultural labourers. In terms of caste composition the Kallars are the largest single group. Among Kallars, Mangalar title holders are numerically dominant. All other caste people come to Kallars for settlement of their disputes. Among the temples Veerapondor Koil is an important centre for religious activities of the village in which 'AMBALAR' is given the 'Prasadam' first as a mark of status first person. Kallars are also trustees of the temple and manage its lands and festivals.

The analysis of the caste and landholding in 1960 shows that both the Kallars and Udayars were dominant economically. However, in 1960 Udayars hand more lands than Kallars, now the situation is other way round. The land distribution is much more dispersed and the persons owning less than 2.5 acres constitute 86 percent of the total land owners. The comparative figures for the district is nearly 80 percent.

External linkages to the village are provided by the institutions like statutory Village Panchayats, Co-operatives and political parties. Interestingly, the Kallars have come to occupy formal positions in these bodies. The prevailing situation regarding party politics shows that the voters are more likely to vote according to their party preferences rather than what the elders of the village say, as was the case earlier. The mass media also seems to have contributed to the political awareness of the voters. The election campaigns seem to have changed from one of mass mobilisation and contact at a place convenient to the voters to contacting them at their doorsteps.

Thus, these features of the study village provide the setting for analysis of sources of power and power holders which are the subject of discussion in the subsequent chapters.

NOTES AND REFERENCE

1. The tables on cropping pattern were based on the data extracted from the land records of the panchayat.
2. Pannaiyal-Permanent agricultural labour who are paid in kind and cash.
3. *Census of India* 1991.
4. Title Holders or Pattapeyar-Each Kallar clan assumes a hereditary title through which blood relations are identified for the purpose of marriage etc.
5. Similar observation was made by Beterille, See Andre Beteille, *Caste, Class and power: Changing Patterns of Social Stratification in a Tanjore village* (Berkly:University of California Press, 1965), p.84.
6. Nicholas B. Dirks, *The Hollow Crown: Ethnohistory of an Indian Kingdom* (Cambridge: Cambridge University Press, 1987), pp. 270-273.
7. *Census of India* 1981.
8. This information was collected through many rspondents. However, at present village land records show the lands against Veerpondor temple. Interestingly the tank under which the lands of the temple is situated is called Mangala

Kulam. At present both Udayars and Kallars cultivate these lands and share the produce with temple.

9. This dispute occurred in the beginning of eighties between two factions of Kallars over their theft of Murugan idol from temple in which one faction accused of others of the theft. This led to irregular conducting of the temple festival in the subsequent years. The details of the dispute is given in the later part of the study.
10. Dirks also observed similar tradition in other parts of the district. Nicholas B. Dirks, op.cit., pp.298-305.
11. See for the details of the rituals associated with visiting of Ayyappan temple Lars Kjaerholm "Myth, Pilgrimage and Fascination in the Ayyappa Cult: A view from field work in Tamil Nadu", in Asko Paropola and Bent Smidt Hamsen (eds.), *South Asian Religion and Society*" (New Delhi : DK, 1986), pp. 121-161.
12. The tables on landholdings were formulated based on the land records of Udayallipatti Panchayat.
13. M.R. Barnett, "Cultural Nationalist Electoral Politics in Tamil Nadu", in M. Weiner and J.O. Field, *Electoral Politics in the Indian States: Party System and Cleavages* vol. iv (Delhi:Manohar, 1975), pp. 78-83.
14. *G.O. MS. Order No. 13* dated 18-1-1986, Rural Development Department, Government of Tamil Nadu.
15. The researcher also observed similar practise in the tea shops situated in other surrounding villages.

Sources of Power : An Analysis

Having presented the broad contours of the Panchayat village and its people in the preceding chapter this chapter focuses on different sources of power with regard to the study area so as to see what sources lead to what kind of power formation. In other words, the sources are studied to see who depends on what sources of power. It is necessary to study different sources of power as it is contended earlier that the power of individuals is, by and large, based on their institutional bases such as caste, landholding, formal institutions or party patterns. It may be possible that a particular leader/power holder has one or many sources of power. The study considers caste, size of landholding, institutions like statutory Panchayat, Co-operatives and political party as sources of power.

1) CASTE STRUCTURE

There are mainly two aspect to be considered regarding caste as a source of power. Firstly, composition in terms of numerical strength of different castes which is important in understanding relative strength of one or more castes. Secondly, inter-caste relationship in terms of hierarchy and the role of 'Ur' panchayat.[1] The Kinship network and unity of different castes are relevant for both the aspects.

a) Numerical Strength

Some scholars consider numerical preponderance of a particular caste as a source of power. For Srinivas numerical preponderance of a caste is one of the elements of dominance.[2] Beteille is of the opinion that a particular caste being numerically preponderant finds high representation in the various panchayati Raj tiers.[3] However, Gardener[4] considers that while numerical strength is a necessary condition of dominance, it is not a sufficient condition. In a similar vein Dube comments that numerical strength, while it is an element of dominance, does not necessarily make a caste dominant.[5] According to Dumont, numbers have a bearing in modern times i.e., elections, but the 'numbers can be made up by members of a clientele more surely than by the members of the dominant caste, among whom there would probably be rivalries of 'factions' once they are numerous'.[6] There appears to be no agreement among different scholars one the role of numerical strength of a particular caste as a source of power. In this context, the following section discusses about the situation obtained from the Udayallipatti Panchayat.

As it described in the previous chapter that Udayallipatti Panchayt is a multi-caste settlement. There were 379 Households with 1337 voters as on 1988 in the Panchayat. Among all the castes, Kallars constitute the Largest group with 127 households and 494 voters sharing 37 percent of votes. As noted earlier, among Kalars, there are different clans like Manglars, Mattayars, Ulaganthar, Palandor etc., identified through different titles. Among different title holders within Kallar caste families with Mangalar title are numerically dominant as the group with 43 households and 147 voters. They are believed to be original clan or settlers among the Kallars or a kind of sons of the soil. In Alwanpatti settlement, kallars with Matters title are numerically dominant. There are more in numbers in this settlement than in the main village. This numerical strength of particular title holders, as it shall be seen later, seems to have a bearing on the power formation.

If Kallars are the largest single group what about other groups ? The table 4.1 shows the details in the order of strength of each group. Among other groups Udayars are largest in number with sixteen percent of votes. Next Konars and Pusaris posses nine percent of votes and other castes have less than nine percent of votes each. However, all of them together possess sixty three percent of votes more than that of Kallars.

Table 4.1 : Numerical strength of caste groups other than Kallars in 1988

S. No.	*Caste*	*No. of house-holds*	*No. of votes*	*Percentage to total votes*
1.	Udayar	60	206	16
2.	Konar	36	125	09
3.	Pusari	34	120	09
4.	SC	32	106	08
5.	Asari	26	87	07
6.	Gounder	27	79	06
7.	Others	37	120	08
	Total	**252**	**843**	**63**

Since the first Panchayat elections in 1958 political power, as manifested in the election of Presidents of Panchayat, has been with the Kallars. The first President who had three terms as president was a Kallar. The second President was also a Kallar. Interestingly, both Presidents belong to Mangalar clan which claim to have originally settled in the village. Both of them belonged to one of the three 'Karais', about which there was a mention in the earlier chapter in the section on Kallars. Interestingly, not only the Presidents but all the contestants were Kallars. The table 4.2 highlights this aspects.

Table 4.2 : Caste background of Presidents and Contestants since 1958 Panchayat elections in the Udayallipatti Panchayat.

Year of Panchayat elections	*President and his caste*	*Contestant and his caste*
1958	HM (Kallar)	BM (Kallar)
1963	HM (Kallar)	QM (Kallar)
1976	HM (Kallar)	QM (Kallar)
1986	QM (Kallar)	HM (Kallar)

From the table 4.2 it can be derived that Kallars, the largest single group, were able to capture and retain formal political power. It is interesting to note that all the Presidents and contestants belonged to one of the three Karais of Mangalars. Despite other major caste groups together possessing more than 50 percent of the votes they could not even put up, let alone win a candidate for the post of Panchayat President in all these elections. Even in the 1986 Panchayat elections nobody else contested from the other castes, only the traditional contenders i.e., Mangalars from kallars caste contested the elections.

In the direct elections for the post of President in 1986, the three terms president, HM got 454 votes while his opponent QM got 536 votes. The whole village was divided into two voting camps. This situations seems to be applicable by and large to the wider area of other village Panchayats in the Kunnondorkoil Panchayat Union. The Table 4.3 illuminates the relationship between Presidents and their caste background.

Table 4.3 : Details of 38 Village Panchayats and Castes of different Panchayat Presidents of Kunnondorkoil Panchayat Union (1986–1990)

S. No.	*Name of the Village Panchayat*	*Caste of each Panchayat President*
1.	Andakulam	Muslim
2.	Chettipatty	Kallar
3.	Kannankudi	Kallar
4.	Kiranur (Town Panchayat)	Kallar
5.	Killanur	Kallar
6.	Killukottai	SC
7.	Killukualvaipatti	Kallar
8.	Kulathur	Kallar
9.	Koppampatty	Konar
10.	Lakknapatty	Kallar
11.	Mangthevanpatty	Kallar
12.	Melapuduvayl	Kallar
13.	Minnathur	Kallar
14.	Mootampatty	Kallar

Contd.

Table 4.3 : (Contd.)

S. No.	*Name of the Village Panchayat*	*Caste of each Panchayat President*
15.	Nanjur	Christian Udayar
16.	Odugampatty	Kallar
17.	Odukkur	Kallar
18.	Palluthupatty	Kallar
19.	Pappudayanpatty	Kallar
20.	Perambalur	Christian udayar
21.	Periyathambi Udayanapatty	Kallar
22.	Pulliyur	Christian Udayar
23.	Rakkathampatty	Kallar
24.	Sennayakkudy	Kallar
25.	Sengalur	Hindu Udayar
26.	Thayinepatty	Kallar
27.	Themmavur	Kallur
28.	Thenuankudi	Hindu Udayar
29.	Taluk Kilayur	Kallar
30.	Udayallipatti	Kallar
31.	Uppiliyakudi	Muthuraja
32.	Vaithuratty	Kallar
33.	Valamangalam	Muslim
34.	Valiampatty	Kallar
35.	Vathna Kottai	Kallar
36.	Vathna Kurichi	Kallar
37.	Veerakudi	Kallar
38.	Visalur	Chettiar

The above data is presented in a different form in the Table 4.4 for further understanding of the situation.

The Table 4.4 suggests that 25 Panchayat Presidents out of 38 belonging to Kunnondorkoil Panchayat Union Hail from Kallar caste. Except two persons from lower caste and two Muslims all the Presidents are from upper and middle level caste. Despite varying strength in different villages, Kallars could win the posts of Presidents in a majority of the Panchayats.

Table 4.4 : Details of the number of Panchayat Presidents from each caste (1986–1990)

S. No.	*Caste of Presidents*	*No. of Presidents*	*Percentage*
1.	Kallar	25	65
2.	Udayar (Christian)	04	10
3.	Udayar (Hindu)	02	05
4.	Agamudayar	01	03
5.	Konar	01	03
6.	Chettiar	01	03
7.	Muthuraja	01	03
8.	SC	01	03
9.	Muslim	02	05
	Total	38	100

General enquiries were made into the surrounding Panchayat like Koppampatti, Rakkathampatty, Vathnakottai, Odugampatti, Killukulavaipatty, Killanur, Minnathur and Taluk Kilayur to know whether, the Presidents belong to largest single groups among Kallars with one particular title holder claiming original settlers status among Kallars. It revealed that like in udayallipatti the Kallars of these Panchayats are numerically strong (though exact percentages are not known) and the Presidents are from title holders which claim original settlers status. Further, contests in these Panchayats for the President's post has been confined only to the Kallars.

Despite this situation in Killukottai and member of the SC community became the President in the 1986 Panchayat elections, though in earlier terms Kallars were Presidents. In the 1986 elections it was reported that there were two Kallars, three Christian Udayars and one SC in the fray. SC candidate was put up after this caste reached an understanding with another lower caste—Muthurajas, who pledged their support for the SC candidate. As votes of Kallars and Udayars got distributed among different candidates of their caste, the SC candidate had won, Mencher also reported in his study on Chengulpet district in Tamil Nadu that in one of the Village Panchayats in the directly contested Panchayat President elections, a member of the SC become the President.[7]

In another Panchayat a Brahmin was the Panchayat President until 1974. Enquiries revealed that it was a Brahmedya village and he was owning most of the lands. This kind of situation, where a small number of Brahmins owned large quantity of local land, they are able to exercise dominance in village affairs. According to Srinivas[8] this kind of situation is an exceptional one. In the 1986 elections, there was a multi-cornered contest between the candidates from Christian Udayars and Kallars in which Christian Udayar won. In the 1986 elections, the President from Brahmin caste did not contest for the elections as he had by then sold off most of his lands.

Enquiry regarding the caste background of Panchayat union Chairman revealed in 1986 elections it was a Kallar from Ambalar family from adjacent Themmavur Panchayat who won the elections and all the contestants were from Kallar caste. The study conducted by Karuppayan in the ten statutory Panchayats in Thanjavur district found that six Presidents out of ten are from the Kallar caste. Further, he concludes that Kallar clan which is a dominant group in the traditional Village Panchayats of a Kallar Nadu has also emerged as a dominant group in the statutory Village Panchayats.[9]

Thus, with the varying numerical strength the persons from Kallar caste have come to occupy formal positions not only in the Udayallipatti Panchayat but also inmost of the Panchayats in the Panchayat Union. About this aspect, Beteille comments that often a particular caste is highly represented in the Village panchayat or the Panchayat Samiti and the Zilla Parishad. This high representation, according to him, may be at times due to the caste in question is preponderant and highly represented in the population as a whole.[10]

At this stage of analysis it is sufficient to point out that Kallars are the only largest single group though they do not have an absolute majority of their own. However, they are able to win the Panchayat elections in 1970 and 1986. This being the case, how was it possible for Kallars to capture the post of President? What is the relationship between the numerical strength and power holders from the Kallar caste? This would be dealt at a later stage in the chapter on Transformation of power.

Kallars are not only dominant numerically whereby they acquire positions in village Panchayat, but also in inter-caste relationship derived from social ranking, land holding, Ur panchayat and religious activities of the village as evident from the following discussion.

b) Inter-caste Relationship:

Different castes interact with one another in the domains of economy, politics, religion etc. The inter-caste relationship is still defined by ritual ranking and hierarchy though not as strictly and rigorously as it was even thirty or forty years ago. For social and ritual position, still different caste people identify and claim themselves to be superior to others, though not all claims are recognised by others.

In the selected Panchayat village, caste groups are more or less in congruence with economic categories -Kallars, Udayars and Konars and Gounders are mostly land owners and cultivators who can be placed in the higher social and ritual ranking. The servicing castes like Asaris, Vannars, etc., though own lands and cultivate, can be placed in the middle of the hierarchy. The lowest ranking castes are Pusaris and Paraiyars (SC)—largely agricultural labourers working for both Udayars and Kallars. A noted feature of the village is the absence of Brahmin and Chettiar caste families. Of course, there were a few Brahmin and Chettiar families earlier. In fact, a few Chettiar families owned lot of lands in the main village and probably this promoted one elderly Kallar respondent to say that the whole village was a Chettiar village. The 1960 land record also confirms this assertion though Chettiars did not own them as extensively as they had before 1960. The table 4.5 places different castes in terms of their social position and occupational divisions.

The classification attempted above is applied in a general way as landowners are present in all the caste groups. However, agricultural labourers are mostly from the lower castes than the

Table 4.5 : Social Position and Occupational Divisions of Different Castes

Social Position	Main Occupation
<u>Upper</u> : Udayar, Kallar, Konar, Gounder	Cultivation
<u>Middle</u> : Asaris, Egali, Navithar	Service
<u>Lower</u> : Pusari, SC	Agricultural Labour

middle and upper ones. According to 1990 village revenue survey there were 25 landless families out of which ten belonged to SC.[11]

The cultivators like Kallars and Udayars possess most of the lands in the village and so other castes particularly persons from SC and Pusari caste are dependent on the former for employment.[12] Earlier, permanent labour through Pannaiyal system was in vogue and permanent labour mainly came from the caste of Pusari and SC. Now by and large that system has disappeared. One Udayar complained that now a days they cannot get Pannaiyals like his father used to get as they go to nearby towns or Caurvery delta for employment. Some of the Udayar boys interviewed said that their parents stopped them from going to school because Pannaiyals from lower castes are no longer available and hence they had to take care of their cattles and subsequently lands. A prominent Kallar leader who owns more than 15 acres of land also complained about lack of labour availability particularly wage labour. It is relevant to recall here that of late lower castes people migrate temporarily to nearby towns and Cauvery delta partly because of lack of rains resulting in less employment opportunities in the village. However, it was reported that some Kallars do have some Pannaiyals to work in their lands. The overall situation is that even though the Pannaiyal system had practically disappeared the service castes and agricultural labourers are still dependent on Kallars and Udayars for employment.

In the village, the social segregation is not as rigorous as before between the cultivating and the servicing caste. Inter-caste marriages are a rare occurrence. Each caste perpetuate their own identity and exclusiveness through marriages among themselves though some of them may interdine. This situation is not applicable when it comes to Pusaris and SCs though Pusaris are treated better and ranked above compared to SCs. The Pusaris can now atleast enter and eat in upper caste houses but not the SCs. Earlier they were not allowed in the 'Ur' streets to walk with foot wear, to cycle or to put towels on their shoulders. As one key Kallar leader put it:

"Earlier they were 'adimais' (slaves) for us. They had to keep their towels under the armpit. Now they put it on the shoulders".

In the similar vein some other upper caste respondents expressed their opinions about the position of SCs now. The discriminatory practices have disappeared over a period of time.

The turning point must have been, as some elder respondents recollected, when Congress party leaders (though exact year was not recollected by the respondents) conducted 'Samabanthi' feast in the village and asked SCs to enter the temple. However, Paraiyars do not enter all the temples still and participate in the temple festivals from outside. Interestingly, a person from SC is a priest for some shrines as mentioned in the earlier chapter, which are located in the west of the main village. Further, in the 'tea shops' in the village, there are separate stainless steel cups and tumblers for SCs and Pusaris. For other caste people tea is served in glasses.[13] Thus, the social barriers against SCs are not as formidable as it was the practice earlier. The remnants, however, are still noticeable in practice.

Thus, in the caste system as it operates in the village now where Kallars, Udayars, Konars and Gounders are placed socially in a higher position than the other castes. However, Kallars are dominant among them as evident from Kallars taking lead in conducting 'Ur' panchayats whether for inter-caste or intra-caste disputes or issues involving the common village interests like temple festivals. Referring to settlement of disputes Srinivas comments that the leaders of dominant caste not only settle dispute between members of different castes but also frequently approached by other castes for the settlement of their internal, even domestic, disputes.[14]

Though all four castes are positioned hierarchically at the top, three castes viz., Udayars, Konars, and Gounders take the matters concerning intra-caste and inter-caste to the Kallars. In the village each caste generally has its own elders to solve their disputes. If it is possible to solve problem of their own they would adjudicate the disputes. Mostly disputes occurring within caste and inter-caste would go to Kallar leaders like PNM, QM, HM, etc. Generally Kallars take the lead in solving the problems. Out of all castes, Kallars and SCs have strong caste panchayat of their own. Even Udyars, though socially and economically equal to Kallars, take their disputes to Kallars. For that matter Gounders from Sathrapatti and Konars from Alwanpatti call on caste and village leaders-Kallars of Udayallipatti-to solve the dispute.

The researcher was a witness to one such panchayat where PNM and QM were adjudicating a dispute between Asari families.

Both the families fought over some family problems and subsequently they approached PNM and QM for adjudicating the dispute. Both PNM and HM stated during the course of the interview with them that other caste people approach them for adjudication. In another case involving a boy and a girl from different religious groups (which happened during the time of field work) the Kallars called 'Ur' panchayat and settled the dispute.

The Udayars take their disputes to Kallars because there was a kind of patron-client relationship (jajmani system) between Udayars and Kalllars earlier in the village, though it is no longer practised residues of it are still left in the inter-relationship between Udayars and Kallars. It is known as co-conut offering by Udayars to Kallars. Each Udayar family has a Kallar or Kallars to conduct ritual offering of co-conut once in a year. This ensures in times of financial distress of a Kallar respective Udayar offers him help and in turn Kallar protects the Udayar family and his property from theft from Kallar gangs. Though it is not practised now, every Udayar still has his own Kallar, who is referred to as 'my Kallar'. Because of this kind of relationship between them in case of disputes within their own caste or with other castes, Udayars would approach their own Kallars rather than their caste fellows.

Another reasons for Udayars approaching Kallars is that the former lack unity. As one Udayar commented:

> *"Udayars do not have unity. They are jealous of each other. If they are not jealous they can solve their own problems. If two Udayars fight, each would go to a Kallar leader. This is how we allow our enemies to play into our caste matters".*

Thus, Udayars are dependent on Kallars for even adjudication of disputes involving their own caste persons.

This matter has another dimension as evident from the response of another Kallar: "In case udayars try to get United Kalars see to it that they are divided among themselves".

The researcher asked PNM as to why other castes, including Udayars, approach the Kallars particularly him, for the adjudication of disputes. PNM responded: "Other caste people think good of me and trust me. Even three Karai Kallars will listen to me as I am related to them in different ways and they feel that if I am given some work I will complete it successfully. In 'Ur' panchayat all the caste people have to accept the decision of three karai Kalars."

When asked as to whether Udayars attend and talk anything in the 'Ur' panchayat? PNM responded: "They also talk but they would expect us to express our opinions first'.

The dominance of Kallar caste is not only restricted to intra-caste and inter-caste disputes but also extends to common village matters such as conducting temple festivals annually in different temples, particularly Veerapondor temple.

It is relevant to mention here that the present trustee, TM, is a Kallar leader and the earlier one HM—the first Panchayat President was the trustee for the Veerapondor Koil which is under the control of the State Government. This temple, as mentioned in the earlier chapter, has lands granted by the Pudukkottai kings to Mangalars to take care of the temple affairs. The temple lands fall under a tank which is called Mangalakulam. Further, in the festivals conducted in this temple, Ambalar is still given 'prasadam' first signifying the importance of his position.[15] The second President, as mentioned earlier, belongs to Ambalar family and is still given 'prasadam' first in the festivals conducted in the temple like his father.

As in the 'Ur' panchayat involving disputes, the three Karai Mangalars play a prominent role in the temple activities also. After the theft of Murugan idol from Veerapondor Koil in 1986, festivals could not be conducted regularly as two factions of Kallars had been accusing each other for the theft and one section refused to participate in the festival. Towards the end of the field work of the researcher in 1990, PNM could bring all sections together, mobilised money through donations by cutting and selling trees which were common property resources made new temple car and conducted the festival.[16] In other temples as well Kallars take the lead in conducting the festivals.

Thus, Kallars are playing prominent role in 'Ur' Panchayat and in temple activities. Closely related to numerical strength, caste position and dominance of Kallars in 'Ur' panchayat are the kinship network and unity among the Kallars. The latter aspects seem to be a source of power for Kallars in general and for the leaders from Kallar caste in particular.

c) Kinship network and Unity

Apart from numerical dominance and leadership in caste and common village interest matters, Kallars derive their power from a strong kinship network in the area. They are distributed widely around the study area unlike other castes. Exception to this being SCs and Pusaris who are also widely dispersed throughout the area. However, they are not socially in the higher position and are dependent upon higher caste for their livelihood. It is common even now for Kallar leaders for the village to go to other village for adjudication of caste disputes as well as inter-village matters and vice versa. Apart from strong tradition of informal panchayat, Kallars of the area are related closely by their marriage alliances and in cases of trouble they would call their relatives from the surrounding area.

Apart from strong kinship network, Kallar also have a strong sense of caste unity. Once after hearing about the incidents of factional fights among Kallars, the researcher asked some Kallar respondents for their reactions towards these incidents. They were of the opinion that even if brothers fight among themselves in Kallar caste they will join hands together when it comes to disputes involving Kallars and other castes. Respondents from other caste also expressed their opinions in the same manner. Karuppayan observed, in his study on kinship and polity of Kallars in Thanjavur district of Tamil Nadu that there is a high degree of conflict and quarrel among the collateral agnates in hereditary property and acquiring wealth and power in their day to day life. At the same time, high degree of group solidarity can be observed among the agnates when there are external challenges.[17] Beteille also observes that Kallars of Thanjavur district have a fairly strong sense of internal solidarity.[18] There were disputes among Kallars reported during the course of field work. However, in these disputes they demonstrated their unity. These disputes will be discussed at a later stage.

2) LANDHOLDING PATTERN

a) Landholding and Caste

Land still continues to be an important source of economic power as most of the people rely on agriculture either directly or indirectly. For Dumont "Land is the most important possession, the only recognised wealth and is also closely linked with power over men".[19] For Beteille economic power is based on ownership and control of land.[20] This was true of the Udayallipatti revenue unit, earlier with the lands concentrating in a few hands. This was the situation forty years earlier. According to elderly informants there were a few big landowners which included quite a few Udayars, two Kallars, two Chettiars, a Brahmin and a Muslim. Among the land owning Udayars, MK Udayar had more lands than others including big landowners from other castes. He had a separate irrigation tank called 'MK Udayar tank' and his descendants continue to own the tank and lands, though not to be same extent.[21]

Barring and few Kallars, others did not own much lands, but worked for MK Udayar as well as for a few Chettiar families. Most of the Kallars also worked for the Chettiar households either as labourers or as tenants, mostly the latter. Subsequently, Kallars bought these lands from the Chettiars over a period of time.[22]

In the 1960s, as was noted in the earlier chapter, the Kallars and Udayars as a whole owned 615.60 acres and 664.08 acres respectively. This works out to 24 percent of the total landholding for Kallars and 26 percent for Udayars in the revenue unit. Together they owned 50 percent of the lands (see table 4.6 and graph 4.1).

Table 4.6 : Landholding Position of Kallars and Udayars in 1960 and 1990

Caste	1960		1990	
	Total lands (acres)	%age of total lands owned	Total land owned (acres)	%age of toal land owned
Kallars	615.60	24	859.39	32
Udayars	664.08	26	699.01	26
Total	**1279.68**	**50**	**1558.40**	**58**

There have been changes in landholding pattern and caste as evident from 1990 land record. Kallars have increased their landholdings from 615.60 to 859.39 acres which make it 32 percent of the total lands owned. Udayars have also increased their landholding though not to the extent Kallars have. In 1990, Udayars

*In Percentage

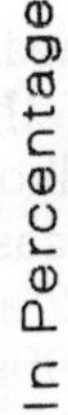

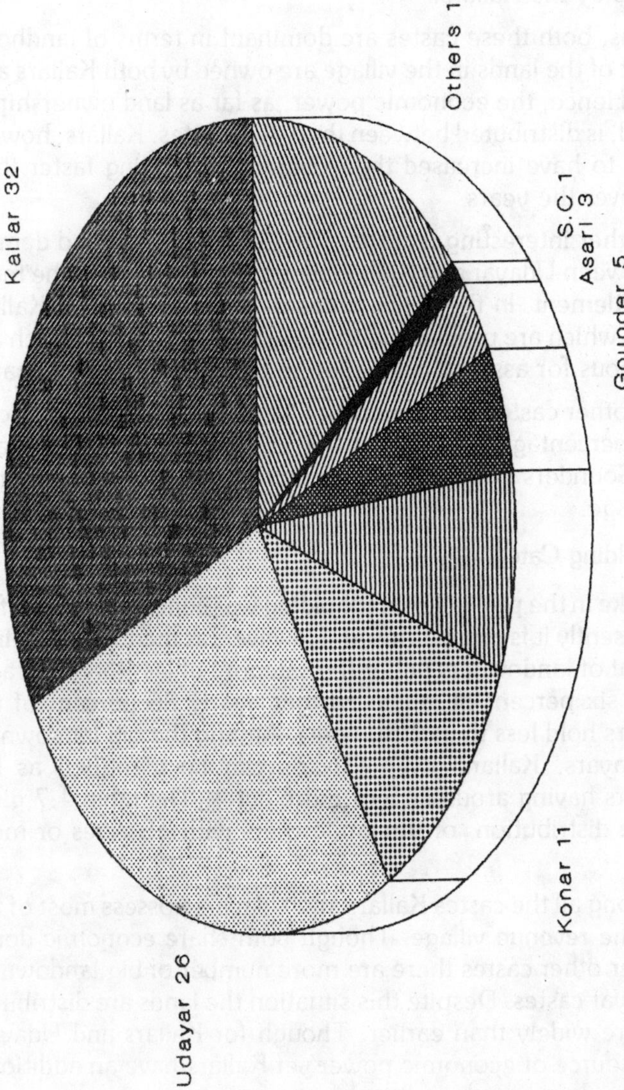

Graph 4.1 : Castewise Landholdings in 1990*
Udayallipatti Panchayat

owned 699.01 acres making it 26 percent of the total lands owned. Together they now have the share of nearly 58 percent of the landholdings (see Table 4.6). Interestingly, despite Kallars having increased their landholding in 1990 Udayars owned on an average 4.72 acres per landowner compared to the average ownership of 2.19 acres by the Kallars.

Thus, both these castes are dominant in terms of landholdings. Most of the lands in the village are owned by both Kallars and Udayars. Hence, the economic power, as far as land ownership is concerned, is distributed between these two castes. Kallars, however, seems to have increased their overall landholding faster than Udayars over the years.

Another interesting feature of landholding is a broad demarcation between Udayar and Kallar lands as it is the case of the main village settlement. In these two areas mostly Udayars and Kallars own lands which are provided with tank irrigation facility which are advantageous for assured cultivation in the normal rainfall years.

For other caste like Brahmins, Chettiars, Muslims their acreage and percentage of lands in the village have decreased and Pusaris, Gounders and Kallars have increased their share of lands in the village.

b) Landholding Categories

Unlike in the past when landholding was concentrated in a few hands presently it is more diffused. However, as mentioned earlier, 43 percent of landowners under the category of less than one acre own only six percent of lands. Further nearly 86 percent of the landowners hold less than 2.50 acres. Among the big landowners some Udayars, Kallars, even Pusaris can be identified as big landowners having around 15 or more acres. The table 4.7 gives caste-wise distribution of the landowners with 15 acres or more acres.

Among all the castes Kallars and Udayars possess most of the lands in the revenue village. Though both share economic dominance over other castes there are more number of big landowners from Udayar castes. Despite this situation the lands are distributed much more widely than earlier. Though for Kallars and Udayars land is a source of economic power yet Kallars have an additional source of power namely political institutions.

Table 4.7 : Caste-wise Distribution of Landowners with 15 or more acres.

S. No.	Caste	No. of Persons
1.	Udayars	10
2.	Kallars	3
3.	Konars	3
4.	Pusaris	1
5.	Chettiars	1
6.	Others	2
	Total	20

3) POLITICAL INSTITUTIONS

The present study deals only with those institutions which have elected representatives such as Village Panchayats and Co-operatives which are sources of administrative, executive and political power.

a) Village Panchayat

The Village Panchayat has formal powers for administrative and developmental activities. The Panchayat President is an executive authority. He can mobilise resources through taxes accrued from various sources and through matching grant from the state government to build a school, panchayat building etc. Further, funds also flow for implementing various developmental schemes. These schemes are implemented by Panchayat Union with the help of various Panchayats under its preview. Another aspect of the village panchayat is the political and social position enjoyed by the President. The Panchayat President is the principal formal link between the village and the development block, it is primarily he who can bring money, work, prestige and modern facilities to the village.[23] During the 1970's Mencher found in another part of Tamil Nadu that this link is crucial one. A majority of Presidents are obviously men with considerable influence and power outside the village. He is another centre of power when he can distribute patronage as well as he can establish linkages with the various government officials by being a member of the Panchayat Union Council. These Linkages can be used for his purposes or for his clients. For instance, through his access to the government machinery he can get loans or subsidies sanctioned for his clients or get various work contracts on his own or somebody's name. It is possible to act like a patron distributing favours to his clients.

Both formal administrative and political powers are, however, subjected to limitations. The formal power in Tamil Nadu, as noted earlier, is subjected to changes or removal from Panchayati Raj bodies by the state government from time to time.

By 1986 most of the subjects of the Panchayat bodies were shifted to respective departments. This forced even Congress (I), an ally of AIADMK, to demand for restoration of powers to Panchayat bodies as originally provided in the 1958 Act. The demand was put forward in the meeting of Panchayt Presidents and Panchayat Union Chairmen called by Congress (I) at Salem in 1986.[24] In the study Panchayat QM complained to the researcher that he cannot even get the fused tubelights replaced by the Electricity Department. Earlier the department was under the control of Panchayats. Same is the case with education, particularly after the primary school teachers were made state government employees accountable to education department and not to Panchayat Unions. Taking of this the previous President HM commented that he could supervise, whether teachers were coming regularly and in case of irregularity he could report the matter to the commissioner (BDO) of Panchayat Union. At present, as they are out of Panchayat Union's control, they are not afraid of Panchayat Presidents. In effect the lack of power affect the functioning and the image of the President.

Despite this situation for the Panchayat bodies in the period 1986-90, getting work contracts for various purposes like roads, buildings, strengthening tank bunds etc., continues to be one of the sources of power for Panchayat President. He can earn money either by taking the work himself or on somebody else name. This was evident from the response of a Christian Udayar President from another Panchayt. He said:

"Now a days there are no powers for a Panchayat President. The only power and source of earning money is through contracts".[25]

Though President were allowed to take work contracts upto a certain amount it is common in the study Panchayat that the Presidents or their clients took various contracts beyond this amount. Thus, being a Panchayat President brings in some power though it is not to an appreciable degree. As far as political power is concerned, it is derived by a persons capacity to initiate and mobilise resources, getting various schemes for the villages, getting contract for oneself on somebody's name or for his clients. However, these sources are subjected to elections to Panchayats being conducted regularly.

To recapitulate, both the Panchayat Presidents elected so far are from Kallar caste with Mangalar title. In the indirect elections HM managed town by mobilising members on panchayat board in his favour. In the direct elections in 1986 though HM lost to QM, the difference was only marginal. One of the reasons for HM losing the 1986 panchayat elections was a few Kallar families shifting their support from HM to QM. They felt that he was deriving 'benefit' from the post. It was, however, not possible to establish these charges. Local informants explained that HM was a small farmer when he became the President for the first time. Now he owns around 20 acres of lands bought a new 'pucca' house. It was common for him to take work contracts on somebody else name. Further, he seems to have utilised his official connection and access to information at the Block headquarters for his personal benefits. Recently he has availed a subsidy for planting trees under social forestry scheme meant for the small farmers.

Unlike the tenure of HM, the tenure of QM saw the Panchayat bodies without much of its powers. Some respondents felt that QM is incapable of being a leader. Several informants expressed was that "He (QM) neither 'earns' money for himself nor allows other to 'earn'. One of his closest ally in the 1986 elections commented on a similar line. On the other hand, QM claimed with the researcher "I am an honest man and did not earn money. I given contracts to others". This is true at least in one instance in which he had given the contract for metalling the Themmvur-Udayallipatti road to a prominent SC leader from the main village. However, his son got employed in the noon meal scheme centre though recruitment policy for the scheme states that destitute and widows should be given preference over others in the appointments.[26]

Thus, Kallars have not only become Presidents of Panchayats but have also controlled channels through which government funds flow to the village. It is doubtful whether Kallars as a whole benefited from the various schemes. It is likely that the Presidents derived benefits from their position. In this regard, one Kallar respondent commented:

"These people (Kallar leaders) approach us for votes in the name of caste and kinship. Once they come to power they do not bother about us. Even if we approach them for some personal work, they say that they will look into the matter but they would never do anything for us."

b) Co-operatives

Unlike Panchayats, Co-operatives such as Primary Agriculture Credit Society, Milk Co-operative Society and Sheep Breeders Co-operative Society, the Presidents of these co-operatives have not come necessarily from the study Panchayat as jurisdiction of these is not restricted to one Panchayat. One Kallar with the Palandor title from the main village was President, during 1969-75, of the Primary Agriculture Credit Society. However, It is only Kallars of the area who have been elected as Presidents of these societies except for a Muslim who was the President of Primary Agriculture Credit Society for one term. In the case of Milk Co-operative Society, and Sheep Breedrs Co-operative Society it is a Kallar with Mattayar title who has held the position of President for two terms. He belongs to Alwanpatti settlement though not from the main village. The dominance of Kallars in the Co-operatives seems to be true at least in the adjacent area. In the adjacent Rakkathampatty, a Kallar was a President for the Milk Cooperative society. In the 1990 elections for this society another Kallar has become the President. Interestingly out of 20 elected directors only two were Kallars and the rest of them were from SC.

Like in Panchayat, President of Co-operatives can distribute favours with his formal and informal powers like getting loans of his clients to buy milch animals etc. The well knows and recent case is that of WMR. He was one of the person who with his familiarity and informal connections with official machinery and banks could get loans from banks for even others to buy milch animals. As result of this when he contested the election for the post of President of these societies, he could win without much contest. In the elections for Milk Co-operatives conducted in 1990, he won against a person belonging to Konar caste. This Konar caste candidate was supported by some Kallar leaders from Udayallipatti. Fearing defections from his camp, WMR took some directors who got elected members to Coimbatore and brought them back a day before the elections.[27]

4) Party Politics

The position in the political parties provides for another external political linkage for the leaders at the village level. There are two ways in which political power could be derived through a position in the party, on the one hand, through the process of mobilization of votes either through local or factional leaders[28] or direct appeal to voters, or personalities.[29] In the process local leaders may emerge as a link between various political parties and the voters. On the other hand, whatever may be their base in their area through identification or holding party position, particularly ruling party, some persons may acquire political power.

It is easy to identify political leaders at the village level on the basis of the party posts they held or if they are MPs or MLAs. However, it is difficult to verify the claims of some individuals who profess that they belong to or they are cadres of a particular party and what power they enjoy in the party. Hence the analysis of party politics and political leaders at the village level is restricted to persons who either held or are presently holding party posts. It is not to deny that persons not holding official position do not exercise any power. Only TM, a Kallar, has held party post as a Union Secretary in AIADMK till 1989. His political territory extends beyond the village boundaries. There are other persons like PHP, a DMK cadre for many years. The Presidents of the panchayat, HM and QM claim themselves as Congressmen. There is another caste leader, SBS, from the scheduled caste who contested the 1989 Assembly elections as an independent candidate unsuccessfully getting only 1011 votes. There are a few young men who are known in the village as AIADMK supporters and some of them are critical of TM because they believe that he has not spent all the money given by the party for election purposes.

It might be said that TM, younger brother of the first President of the Panchayat, who held AIADMK party posts may be considered as a political leader. He started his political career with DMK and left it to join AIADMK when MGR came out from it to start Anna Dravida Munnerra Khazhagam. He held party union Secretary post till 1989. His mentor from the district R M Veerappan, was minister in MGR's cabinet. In the 1989 elections TM was with AIADMK (Janaki) group along with RM Veerapan. Subsequently he shifted his loyalty to AIADMK splinter group led by Thirunavukarasu- a Kallar and a former minister in MGR's cabinet. He won from his constituency, Arantangi (Pudukkottai district) for fifth time in 1991. In the 1991 assembly elections Thirunavukarasu led his own party APTTMK, which won only two seats.

It is most likely that TM held political power because of his formal position as Panchayat Union Secretary, in the party. It is not clear whether he got votes because he belongs to Kallar caste or because of MGR's charisma. It is significant to note that the Kulathar Assembly constituency (reserved) has been returning AIADMK candidates since 1980. In the elections conducted in 1989 and 1991 it returned candidates from AIADMK (Jayalalitha). Thus, it can be inferred that AIADMK has a strong presence in the area.

It is alleged that TM has misused his political position to acquire economic power. It is rumoured widely that he has acquired wealth by using his political connections. He had inherited only a few acres. Subsequently he got lands from his wife's side and was also leasing-in some lands from a Udayar and cultivating them. He also bought a motor cycle, a symbol of prestige in the area, and subsequently sold it off. He has constructed a pucca house and bought a thatched house in the part of the village which is considered to be the area of Udayars. His rapid prosperity lends credibility to the widely held rumours.

It was well known that he used his party position to get contract for many arrack shops at a lesser rate and was running them through intermediaries. Few years back it was reported by some AIADMK cadres of the village that he promised some young men he would get jobs for them in police department and collected some money. Though he had promised ten persons he could get the jobs only for three. It was reported that he has not returned the money to the rest. Further, some AIADMK youth accused him of not spending all the money given by the party during the elections.

SUMMING UP

From the above analysis of different sources of power, the

following conclusions can be drawn: Kallars - the largest single group were able to acquire formal village Panchayat position so far. Other castes, though possess fifty percent of votes, have not been able so far to challenge Kallars in capturing formal Panchayat positions. Kallars not only have captured and retained formal political power in Udayallipatti Panchayat but also in most of the panchayats of the Kunnondorkoil Panchayat Union. The Kallars of the area were able to win in 25 out of total 38 Panchayats in the 1986 Panchayat elections. Interestingly only persons from mangalar clan and not Kallars from other clans were able to contest the Panchayat elections so far.

Apart from numerical strength, Kallars derive their power from inter-caste relationship. Though socially Kallars are placed on par with Udayars, Gounders and Konars the latter lack sufficient numerical strength and unity among themselves to challenge Kallars. They are dependent on Kallars for solving both intra-caste and inter-caste disputes. Kallars are not only approached by other caste persons but also Kallars on their own take the lead in these matters. Apart from dominance of Kallars in 'Ur' Panchayat they also dominate temple activities of the village. It is necessary to note here that all the trustees in recent years for main temple of the village belong to Kallar caste and particularly from Mangalar clan. In the main temple Veerapondor Koil Ambalar from Kallar caste is given 'prasadam' first as a symbolic recognition of his status of first person in village. Generally Kallars take lead in conducting festivals in most of the temples of the village. The dominance of Kallars in internal politics might be linked to kinship network and unity among Kallars.

As far as land as a source of power, Udayars and Kallars together possess most of the lands in the village thereby making other castes dependent on them for work and employment. Between Udayars and Kallars, Kallars as a whole possess more lands than the Udayars though land-man ratio is more favourable in the case of Udayars than Kallars. Unlike the earlier situation, at present the distribution of land is much more diffused. However, overall Kallars and Udayars are dominant economically in the Panchayat village.

Kallars apart from possessing these sources of power also occupy formal position Panchayat and Co-operatives. In the formal institutions like Panchayat, the President commands both formal and informal powers. Formal powers include both administrative and developmental activities. Informal powers include both political and social influences the post brings for the President. It provides a link to the world outside the village. However, these powers are subjected to regularity of elections conducted to these bodies and devolution of powers by the state government, which in turn affects the performance and image of the President. In recent times, however, getting work contracts seems to be an important benefit the office holder get from his position.

As in Panchayat, in Co-operatives also Kallars have come to occupy important positions and the President can help his clients through the benefits flowing through these institutions.

Party politics provides another external linkage with the outside world. And also identifying with the party in power brings power to the person. In the study village a Kallar had been Union Secretary for AIADMK in the eighties. He seems to have benefited by this political connections.

After having analysed the sources of power for identifying the persons who are holding power, it is necessary to discusses about the other aspect of power formation i.e., power holders.

NOTES AND REFERENCES

1. The terms 'Ur 'panchayat refers to informal village panchayat where elders of the village settle disputes between persons or groups. It is also called for whenever there is matter of common concern of the village arises like conducting of temple festivals.
2. M.N. Srinivas, *The Dominant Caste and Other Essays* (Delhi: Oxford, 1987), p.97.
3. Andre Beteille, *Caste, Class and Power : Changing Patterns of Social Stratification in Tanjore village* (Barkley : University of California Press, 1965).
4. Peter M. Gardner, "Dominance in India : A Reappraisal". *Contributions to Indian Sociology* New Series No. II. 82-97,

1968.

5. S.C. Dube, "Caste Dominance and Factionalism", *Contributions to Indian Sociology* New Series No. II, 58–81, 1968.
6. L. Dumont, *Homo Heirarchicus : An Essay on the Caste System* (Chicago : University of Chicago Press, 1980), p.162.
7. Joan P. Mencher, *Agriculture and Social Structure in Tamil Nadu: Past Origins, Present Transformations and Future Prospects* (New Delhi : Allied, 1978), p. 274.
8. M.N. Srinivas, op. cit., p.8.
9. V. Karuppayan, *Kinship and Polity : A Study in Socio-political Organisation among the upland Kallars of Thanjavur District in Tamil Nadu* (Madras : Madras University Press, 190), p. 99.
10. Andre Beteille, *Caste : Old and New, Essays in Social Structure and Social Stratification* (Bombay : Asia Public House, 1969), p. 154.
11. Information derived from discussion with Village Administrative Officer in 1989.
12. L. Dumont, op. cit., p.106.
13. This was observed not only in the surrounding villages but also in a town like Kirnaur - the taluk headquarters of the Udayallipatti Panchayat.
14. M.N. Sriniwas, op. cit., pp. 102-115.
15. Nicholas B. Dirks, *The Hollow Crown: Ethnohistory of an Indian Kingdom* (Cambridge : Cambridge University Press, 1987), pp. 298-305.
16. The researcher has witnessed one such situation where PNM was supervising the felling of few remaining trees of the bunds of the village common pond to be used for temple festival purposes.
17. V. Karuppayan, op.cit., pp. 39-40.
18. Andre Beteille, op.cit., pp. 84-85.
19. L. Dumont, op. cit., p. 156.
20. Andre Beteille, op. cit., pp. 143-144.
21. The property of M.K. Udayar was distributed among his two

daughters which then subsequently to their descendants.

22. This process took many years as evident from the village land records of 1960 and 1990.
23. Joan P. Mencher, op. cit., p. 272.
24. M.B.L. Muthayya, *Panchayat Union Administrations (Tamil)* (Madras : New Century Book House, 1986), p. 142.
25. This conversation took place in a tea shop in Kunnondorkoil _ block headquarter - after the respondent tried for contract which was auctioned at that day in the Panchayat Union Office.
26. Barbarra Harriss, *Child Nutritions and Poverty in South India* (New Delhi : Concept , 1991), pp. 69-70.
27. The researcher happened to be present at the day of elections in nearby Kunnondorkoil where it was observed that WMR was providing hospitality to the officer who was to conduct the elections.
28. M.J. Barnett, "Cultural Nationalist Electoral Politics in Tamil Nadu," in Myron Weiner and J.O. Field, *Electoral Politics in the Indian States : Party System and Cleavages* Vol. I (Delhi: Manohar, 1975), pp. 78-83.
29 John Harriss, *Capitalism and Peasant Farming: Agrarian Structure and Ideology in Northern Tamil Nadu* (Bombay : Oxford University Press, 1986), p. 277.

5 Power Holders : Their Profiles and Sources of Power

In the preceding chapter different sources of power are analysed to find out who has what sources of power. Different sources considered for analysis are caste structure, landholding, formal institutions like statutory Village Panchayat and Co-operatives and political parties. The analysis of these institutional bases of power is in confirmation with the earlier mentioned contention of the study, viz., individual power is to a large extent dependent on institutional power and it is within the institutional framework that the individuals or power holders acquire power. Accordingly emphasis is given on institutional bases of power in the study.

However, attention is also to be paid to other aspect of power formation that is power holders. This is necessary to understand their role in various aspects of power formation. For this purpose, sketch of the profiles of power holders is attempted in this chapter. These profiles focus on caste and social position of power holders, their age, education, landholding, occupation, formal or informal position and political affiliation. With the help of these profiles an attempt is also made to compare the socio-economic background of power holders. This, in turn, would present an overall and comprehensive picture of the power holders in the Panchayat.

Attempt is also made to compare power holders in terms of their sources of power. The sources of power considered for comparison are caste, landholding, statutory Panchayat, Co-operatives and political affiliation. This serves two purposes. In the first place, it is to indicate which person has or had what and how many sources of power. Secondly, it is useful to classify power holders in terms of their internal or external source of power. The study considers caste and landholding as internal while others as external sources.

PROFILE OF HM[1]

HM belongs to Kallar caste with Mangalar title. He is from the main village Udayallipatti. As it was mentioned earlier Kallars with Mangalar title claim to be the original settlers and in turn Mangalar title holders are divided into three 'Karais' (sections). HM belongs to middle Karai. He was around 57 Years at the time of the study. He has three brothers and is the eldest of all. One of his brothers was a Union level Secretary for AIADMK party from 1980 to 1989. His formal education is upto primary level. He is one of the village elders whom village at large including persons from his caste approach for adjudication of disputes. He was the trustee of Sannayasi Koil for a few years.

According to local informants HM was a small farmer 20 years ago and the land records of 1960 also confirm this assertion. At present he owns around 20 acres which include three acres of dry land registered in his son's name. Apart from what he inherited from his ancestral property he has bought nine acres of land from a Brahmin and five acres from a Konar subsequently. He has invested around Rs. 30,000 to dig a well of 20 metres depth which has not yielded sufficient water. He owns two houses one being thatched ancestral house and the other a pucca house just adjacent to SC settlements, which he bought from a Muslim.

He was Panchayat President for three successive terms that is for 15 years since 1958. He was never elected unanimously and there was always contest from other Kallars. First it was from a lower Karai Kallar BM and in the next two terms contest was from an upper Karai Kallar QM. In the fourth Panchayat elections in 1986 HM lost to QM by a margin of 82 votes. Though he lost the election he successfully put up his supporter KMA of Asari caste for the post of vice-president. In the indirect election to the vice-president seven votes were casted in favour of KMA while his opponent got five votes out of total twelve votes.

According to an elderly Kallar respondent, a close confident of HM, the defeat of HM in the 1986 Panchayat elections was a consequence of a quarrel of HM with some Kallars hailing from the main village. Because of this they have shifted their support from HM to QM. This was also brought out during the counting of votes in which HM was leading during the counting of the votes of hamlets of Udayallipatti. The trend, however, was reversed when it comes to counting the votes of the main village. There are other reasons attributed to his failure. Some respondents felt that he was getting 'benefit' out of his position which people resented. Even his closest ally, another prominent Kallar leader PNM, shifted his support from HM to QM. This resulted in the clash between HM's group with another group led by BM and some Palandors who supported the alliance of PNM and QM in 1986 Panchayat elections. In his interview with the researcher, PNM informed:

" He (HM) was not bothering about the poor. You have to take the poor along and do service to them. Further he (HM) stopped hearing my advice though I have been supporting him from the beginning. Hence I decided not to work for him in the Panchayat election. In this condition when QM approached me for my support I agreed to work for him in the elections"

Whatever the reasons for the defeat of HM in the 1986 Panchayat elections he has been able to come to power for three terms. During the elections for these three terms he was never a consensus candidate getting elected unanimously. He always faced opposition, right from the first Panchayat elections in 1958 first from lower Karai Mangalars and subsequently from upper Karai Mangalars, particularly from QM. Not only that, despite opposition from other factions of Kallars he has commanded, according to elderly respondents, support from major sections of Kallars and other castes in the main village. He has also commanded substantial support from the hamlets of the Udayallipatti Panchayat particularly from Gounder and Konar castes. Reasons for his success are manifold. One of them being the wide perception of his leadership capacities, his ability to get things done both at local and block levels, the lead provided by him in conducting 'Ur' panchayat and in common village matters like mobilisation of men and resources for temple festivals etc. Other caste people also approach him on their own to settle their disputes. He is one of the caste elders who sits in 'Ur' Panchayat.

During his tenures as Panchayat President there were many development works undertaken, some with the financial contribution from the Panchayat and some without it. These include construction of Panchayat building, Radio room, Water tank, digging of an open well, laying of pipeline for supply of drinking water. Apart from these there were programmes of laying new roads or improving the old ones, strengthening of tank bunds and renovation of sluices. HM in the interview with him claimed that during his three terms as the President, the Panchayat spent nearly Rs. 75,000 on various public works. When the Panchayats were dissolved in 1974 there was a surplus of Rs. 26,000. Further, he claimed that through his personal efforts school building was constructed at the cost of Rs.45,000. It was alleged that in some of the works which were either undertaken by himself or by some others for him, he earned money through these contracts. According to one Kallar respondent that HM has acquired lot of property after he became the Panchayat President. People in general and in particular those from Udayallipatti felt jealous of his growth though he has done lot of work for the village.

Further, his position as a Panchayat President and a member of the Panchayat Union Council gave him access to various government officials. Through cultivation of these contacts it was possible for him to know about the various rural development schemes, and use it for personal benefits. One such incident, which the researcher came to know was using his contacts to get subsidy earmarked for small farmers to plant causerina trees under social forestry scheme in his lands. It is to be noted here that he owns twenty acres of land.

His political affiliation, he claimed, has been always with the Congress party. He recollected how he was responsible for arranging meetings of Congress leaders like Kamaraj, Rammaya, and Kakkan when they visited the village. He proudly recalled about his garlanding of these leaders.

For HM, being the member of Kallar caste and position as a President in the Village Panchayat for three terms are sources of power. Subsequently he has acquired lands which have become another source of power. He has been active in the village politics for more than three decades. He exercised his power through combination of his caste domination over other castes and his position as the President of the Panchayat. He has also acquired the reputation in the village as one of the persons to solve problems in 'Ur' panchayat. However in the late eighties his position as one of the important persons in the village has declined which will be dealt at a later stage of the study.

PROFILE OF QM

QM is a Kallar with Mangalar title and is from the main village. He represents the upper Karai Mangalars. He was 50 years old and a son of an Ambalar. He is referred to in the village as Ambalar though he enjoys name of the formal authority. His father was elected unanimously as Panchayat President for a few years in the fifties, however, he did not allow his son to contest in the subsequent Panchayat elections. QM's formal education was upto 5th standard.

The assets of QM include a pucca house, 10 acres of land with a well and a diesel engine. His father was one of the big landowners in the village. QM shared his ancestral property with a brother. He has, now, sold some of his property. Commenting on QM's economic position one Udayar respondent informed that QM's father had surplus grains at home throughout the year but now QM buys ration rice.

QM was Panchayat President from 1986 to 1990. He won the election, as mentioned earlier, against HM with a margin of 82 votes. However, he could not succeed in preventing HM's candidate KMA of Asari caste being elected as Vice President of the Panchayat board.

Some respondents commented that he is not an effective President. It may be partly because by 1986 most of the powers had been taken away from the village Panchayats. For instance, school teachers have been taken out of the local bodies control and are now placed under Education Department. Likewise, the public health centres in Panchayat Unions have come under Health Department and the State Water and Drainage Board is incharge of all drinking water supply schemes leaving only the distribution to the local bodies. Further people's representatives in local bodies are now not empowered to inspect the Noon Meal Scheme though the buildings are to be maintained by the village Panchayats.

During the discussion with the researcher, QM complained about lack of powers of Village Panchayats. He said that the previous President was allowed to buy and replace the fused street lights and now it is the Electricity Department which does this. He complains that the Electricity Department does not replace the fused lights immediately. Further, he said he has given five petitions to dig one more common well for drinking water supply but has failed to get any response. He was also keen to construct a public platform for political meetings. Commenting on the financial position of the Village Panchayat, he felt that it is difficult to collect house taxes etc., from the people as rains have not been sufficient for some years. He felt that people in general fail to understand the problems faced by him. However, they demand some works to be done. Despite this situation when the contract for digging of wells came people are hesitant to take up as they are not sure of how much money they can make out of this contract.

Some respondents, including one of his supporters who voted for QM in the 1986 Panchayat elections, felt that he is inefficient as he neither 'earns money' nor he allows others to 'earn money' making use of power vested in him. The former contention is difficult to prove, however, the latter is not true at least in one instance where he could have taken the contract of gravelling mud road between Udayallipatti and Themmavur himself instead he has given it to a prominent SC leader of the main village. Nonetheless, it is to be noted that during his tenure he got his son employed as a Noon Meal Scheme supervisor though the recruitment policy for the scheme emphasises on recruitment of destitutes and widows.[2]

QM claimed that he belongs to Congress and in his nomination papers for the 1986 Panchayat elections he has mentioned this political affiliation.

His sources of power are caste and formal position of the Village Panchayat President for one term. His selection to the post appears to be based on negative votes against HM. Though QM is given the status of first person in Veerapondor temple he has not proved himself effective while he was a Panchayat President. Even his allies do not have favourable opinion of his performance.

PROFILE OF TM

TM, aged 45 years, is a Kallar with Mangalar title and is the younger brother of HM. He is educated upto high school. He is the only Kallar in the Udayallipatti Panchayat who has held a post as a Union Secretary in AIADMK. He was also a trustee of the Sannayasi Koil for some years.

At present, according to the land records, he owns fifteen acres of dry and wet lands, and a well with an electric pumpset. When the ancestral property was divided among brothers he got 4 acres of land as his share, subsequently, he got some lands from his wife's side and has also bought more lands. Further, he leased in 6 acres of land from a Udayar which he is yet to return. He has a pucca house constructed in the late eighties and has bought a thatched house in a Udayar area of the village. He owned a Bullet motorcycle (symbol of prestige) for some years which he later sold off.

As mentioned earlier, TM was a Union Secretary in AIADMK party from 1980 to 1989. His political career had ups and downs. He was in DMK in the sixties and came out of it and joined ADMK which was founded by MGR in 1971. He became Union Secretary for Kunnondorkoil Union in AIADMK (ADMK was renamed as AIADMK). In his interview with the researcher TM elaborated on his closeness to his mentor from Pudukkottai district R.M. Veerappan, then a minister in MGR government and his many meetings with MGR. After MGR's death, AIADMK got split into AIADMK (Jayalalitha) and AIADMK (Janaki). His mentor R.M.Veerappan associated himself with Janaki group, TM also followed. After Janaki group failed miserably in the assembly elections in 1989, there was a period of political inactivity for him, until S.Thirunauvkarasu, a Kallar by caste also former minister in MGR's government met him on one occasion and persuaded him to join AIADMK (Jayalalitha). As S.Thirunavukarasu had differences with Jayalalitha and started Anna Puratchi Thalaivar Thamizhaga Munnerra Khazhagam (APTTMK) TM joined the same. In 1991 assembly elections he campaigned for APTTMK which got few seats in the elections.

There have been more than one occasion in which TM used

his political connection to derive benefits. In one instance, he used his connection with R.M. Veerappan to bail him out in a quarrel with other Kallars. The lattergave a police complaint against TM and for that he was arrested by the local police. The local Sub-Inspector of police is believed to have got a telephone call from the Minister to release him.

Further, according to the informants, he has taken on contract ten arrack shops in the area and sub-contracted them, thereby earning by only supervising them. In another case he is said to have promised to get police constable jobs to some young men in the village and collected money. Using his political power he could get the jobs for three persons. However, he neither got the jobs for the others nor returned the money. Local AIADMK youth in their informal discussion with the researcher mentioned that TM had not spent all the money that he got from AIADMK party during the elections.

Apart from his caste as a source of power his formal position as a Union Secretary in AIADMK party has given him another source of power. He has effectively used this source not only to establish his position in the village politics but also appears to have earned money. He lost his link with political power derived through position in political party mainly because of his miscalculated political moves. However, he still plays important role in the village as evident from elections to Co-operatives and in Murugan idol theft case.[3]

PROFILE OF WMR

WMR is a Kallar with Mattayar title and belongs to Alwanpatti, one of the hamlets of Udayallipatti Panchayat. As mentioned earlier Alwanpatti settlement has Kallars predominantly with Mattayar title holders. He was 35 years old at the time of the study and one of the young persons to emerge as power holder in the recent years. He is educated upto to tenth standard. He owns ten acres of both dry and wet lands in Alwanpatti.

WMR was a President of both Milk Co-operative Society and Sheep Breeders Co-operative Society for a term. In the earlier elections conducted in 1985 for these co-operatives he won unopposed. However, in the 1990 elections for Sheep Breeders Cooperative Society a candidate from Konar caste contested against him with the support of Udayallipatti Kallar leaders like HM and TM. These leaders traditionally have been supported by Konars of Alwanpatti.

In the elections WMR won against the candidate from Konar caste. In the subsequent election in the same year for Milk Co-operative Society WMR won against another Konar candidate by reportedly taking away two directors belonging to Gounder caste from Sathrapatti to Coimbatore and bringing them back just a day before the elections. Out of fourteen directors WMR was sure of support from seven according to local informants but not sure of two Gounders. Hence he resorted to removing them from the area, so that they can not be persuaded by his opponents to vote against him. Despite opposition even from other Kallars, he managed to win the elections by getting ten votes one more than what he expected.

WMR was one of the first persons who had taken loans from Banks.for buying milch animals and sheep. With his familiarity with the procedures and experience he has managed to get loans for others in the village. He is also believed to have taken a commission for these transactions.He has earned the loyalties of the persons in the process. Though he got elected unopposed in the earlier term for these societies in the latest elections he faced opposition. This might be because, as one Konar respondent put it, "people have realised the value of these posts".

His main source of power seems to be his formal position in the Co-operatives. Though opposed by his own caste persons from Alwanpatti and Udayallipatti he could win the post in Co-operatives. It is not to say that his position as a Kallar has not helped him.

PROFILE OF SP

SP is a Kallar from Palandor clan and is HM's uncle. He was 61 years old and formally educated upto primary level. His family owns nine acres of both dry and wet lands.

He was the President of Primary Agriculture Credit Society from 1969 to 73. In the next election to the society he lost to another Kallar from adjacent village by two votes. He is the only person so far from the main village to become the President of this Co-operative Society. It may be due to the fact that the area of operation of Co-operative Societies not necessarily confirms to the area of Panchayat village or revenue village. However, it is necessary to point out that for this society so far Kallars from the area of operation of the society have become Presidents exception being a Muslim becoming a President for one term.

During the course of interview with the researcher he elaborated on how he managed to collect outstanding dues without violent methods like removing doors, grains etc. He feels that the use of these methods are counter productive and quoted some instances where officials were beaten up by people which led to police case.

He has acquired his power by being the member of Kallar caste. His formal position in the Primary Agriculture Credit Society is another source of power. However, he lost this source of power when the next elections for Co-operatives took place.

PROFILE OF BM

BM represents the lower Karai head of the Mangalars. He is not formally educated. He is 68 years old. His family owns fifteen acres of both dry and wet lands which include his son's property also and a well with a good supply of water throughout the year. He has an electric motor to irrigate his fields. He is one of the first farmers to install an electric motor in the 1960s. He lives in a pucca house heading a joint family. He claims to be a Congressman.

BM has been opposed to HM and his faction over the years. He contested unsuccessfully against HM in the Panchayat elections in 1958. In the 1986 Panchayat elections he extended his support to QM along with another Kallar leader PNM who also belongs to his Karai. Other clans of Kallars like Palandors and Thethuvandors, who have been opposing the HM faction traditionally also extended their support to QM in the elections. This created a resentment among the HM supporters and their leaders and led to factional fight immediately after the elections in which BM was also involved. In the course of this fight BM and PNM were abused by other faction members led by TM and HM.

BM, though supported QM along with PNM in the elections he felt disappointed with the performance of QM. Once he asked QM about the fused tube lights which needed replacement. He felt the answers given by QM are not satisfactory and neither he could persuade the electricity department to replace nor afford to spend his money and buy them. BM felt, on the other hand, that the earlier President HM is a clever and capable man and he could get many things done for the village like bore well, water tank and Panchayat building, Radio and so on.

Though he has not held any formal position of office so far he is one of the important caste leaders from Kallar caste. He is one of the persons to be called in the event of 'Ur' Panchayat. Further, he has been leading one of the factions which all along opposed to faction led by HM. Though he supported HM in the 1986 Panchayat election he has expressed his unhappiness over the performance of HM. Apart from this he is one of the big landowners from the main village which is another source of power.

PROFILE OF PNM

PNM is a Kallar with Mangalar title and belongs to lower Karai. He is 75 years old and educated upto primary level. He owned lands in the main village some years back. He has now sold his lands in the village and bought seven acres of land in a nearby town. He is settled there, and occasionally makes visits to the main village. He is one of the caste and village leaders to adjudicate disputes involving intra-caste and inter-caste matters, as well as common village affairs. He frequently visits Udayallipatti for conducting temple festivals. It was learnt that he used to take interest in the religious activities of village like construction of temple, conducting festivals etc. The two temples which are located in the centre of the main village (See map III)were constructed mainly because of his efforts. During the course of the field work researcher met him frequently in the main village adjudicating a dispute between two sections of Kallars over the theft of Murugan idol from Veerapondor Koil. This theft took place in 1982 and since then festivals of this temple could not be conducted regularly with the participation of all sections of Kallars. PNM was persuading both the sections of Kallars to compromise on this issue. This dispute extended over eight years which he could successfully resolve and conduct the festival in 1990.

PNM claimed in his interview that three Karai Kallars would listen to him as he was elderly and experienced in settling the disputes. Further, they are all related to him. He said that not only three Karai Kallars but other caste people as well approach him for solving their problems. This version was confirmed by other caste people including Gounders, Udayars, Konars, Pusaries, SCs etc. As noted earlier the other caste people generally approach Kallars for solving their disputes in particular PNM, QM and HM. The researcher has witnessed one such panchayat where QM and PNM were adjudicating an Asari family dispute. Apart from this dispute, PNM was one of the persons to call for 'Ur' panchayat in a dispute involving youth from different religions. This panchayat was important as it met after a long time and all the factions of Kallars participated in it. The 'Ur' panchayat could not meet because of factional dispute over Murugan idol theft case. According to PNM he has used this opportunity to initiate a dialogue with the factions involved in the dispute.

As mentioned in the profile of HM, PNM was a long time ally of HM. PNM claimed that he was the one who proposed HM as a candidate in the 1958 Panchayat elections. This relationship lasted till the middle of 1980s. He said that though HM is his close relative frictions developed between them. The main reason is that HM has stopped listening to his advice. Further HM stopped bothering about the poor. This was pointed out to HM which he ignored. PNM felt that "poor should trust us and without their support nobody can be person of importance". It was in this context, just before the 1986 Panchayat elections QM approached him seeking his support. PNM agreed to work for the former in the Panchayat elections.

Subsequently there was factional fight between HM's group and some Palandors and lower Karai Mangalars headed by BM over PNM's shift of support from HM to QM. The details of this factional fight is given in the profiles of QM and BM. PNM political affiliation, as he claimed, has been with Congress.

His power is based on his position as a Kallar and all the more he belongs to one of the Mangalar clan. However he does not seem to be holding as much power as he had earlier. This is evident from his difficulties in getting all the sections of Kallars united in Murugan idol theft case.

PROFILE OF KSU

KSU belongs to Udayar caste and is from the main village. He was 40 years old and is educated upto primary level. He lives in a pucca house. His source of power is his landholding. Among Udayars he is the biggest landowner with 27 acres inclusive of dry and wet lands.

Though he owns lands, like other persons in his caste, he has not held any formal position or office so far. The respondent felt that since the time of MK Udayar no other Udayar has emerged as an important person playing active role in local politics. During the time of MK Udayar, Udayars could unite under him atleast on one occasion. On that occasion it was contested as to who - whether Kallars or Udayars - could offer prayers first to deities at Veerapondor Koil. The Udayars could be able to unite under MK Udayar because not only he was the biggest land owner but also he was holding the post of Karnam. Further, many Kallars were working in his lands. Despite these factors the dispute was resolved finally by compromising that Kallars would offer prayers first and then the Udayars. The respondent felt that though Udayars have better land-man ratio than Kallars they play a subordinate role in local affairs. Though Udayars from his caste are invited and given equal status in 'Ur' panchayat, they do not assert themselves. They react to the problems at hand only after Kallars express their opinion. Like other Udayars KSU has also his own Kallar to fall back upon in case of disputes with his or other caste persons.

The respondent also felt that there is no unity among Udayars themselves for resolving the disputes arising within their caste persons. He also felt that even if Udayars try to unite Kallars would divide them. Though he is the supporter of Congress party he is not an active member of it.

PROFILE OF TSU

TSU is also a Udayar and from the Chinnauranipatti - a Udayars hamlet. He is an illiterate. He was 60 years old. He owns 20 acres of land both dry and wet. He uses electric motor for irrigation. He commands respect in and around the hamlet because of his large landholding.

Like KSU he has not held any formal position in the Panchayat or in any other formal institutions, so far. He attends 'Ur' panchayats but does not play any active role in them. Like other Udayars, he says, he minds his cultivation. He does not have any particular preference for any political party.

PROFILE OF KMA

KMA is a Christian from Asari caste. He was 50 years old and illiterate. He owns 6 acres of dry land. He is blacksmith and owns a workshop in which he makes mainly iron spare parts for bullock-carts in the main village which is an important centre in the area for making these carts. He was a goldsmith to start with but he later changed to blacksmithy. His elder son has become an electrician and another son is helping him in the workshop.

He was Vice President between 1986 and 1990 of the village Panchayat Board. He was the candidate of HM who lost the 1986 Panchayat elections for the post of President. In the indirect elections for vice-president KMA got seven votes and his opponent secured five from twelve member Panchayat Board. Though he belongs to middle level caste he derives his power from his position as a Vice-President of Panchayat.

During the interview with the researcher he was critical of QM and expressed that he is neither honest nor capable of doing things like HM. He expressed that he does not have preference for any particular political party.

PROFILE OF PHP

PHP belongs to what is traditionally known as Valayar caste. This caste is locally referred to as Pusari caste and is officially classified as Muthurajas. His age is around 40 years. He is educated upto primary level. He owns 10 acres of wet and dry lands with a well and a diesel engine. His source of power is his landholding. He lives in a thatched house in Mazhavarayanvayal settlement. He is a prominent person from Pusari Caste. He is known in the village as a committed DMK cadre. He has not held any party position so far. However, his committed position as a cadre in DMK party has given him some standing in the village. He claimed with the researcher to be a principled man and is committed to serve others. Though DMK has been out of power intermittently for many years he has not quit the party.

PROFILE OF SBS

SBS is from Scheduled Caste and is a prominent person from the caste. He is 57 years old. He has four acres of dry and wet lands with a well dug recently under 'Jeewan Thara' scheme. He lives in a pucca house constructed a few years back. He has completed a contract work of laying gravels over mud road between Udayallipatti and Themmavur.

SBS is not formally educated but is very articulate as evident from the researcher's first meeting with him in a tea shop where it took half an hour to convince him about the purpose of the study. Subsequently, in many other interactions the researcher found him articulating his points clearly. On one occasion in a teashop in the Block Headquarters he was impressing upon a clerk from Block Development Office about how his pending file should be cleared. In the process he commented:

"I am not supposed to talk because I am going to Sabarimalai temple (devotees of Ayyappan are not supposed to talk much). But if I do not talk(articulate) my work will not be done."

That seems to be his strength. He claimed with the researcher that he is a religious person. In 1990 it was his third visit to Sabarimalai Ayyappan temple. He was seen participating with other caste people in the bhajans conducted by Ayyappan devotees in Kunnandorkoil. He was also respectfully called by other devotees as 'SB swamy[4].

In one of the discussions, he mentioned about his efforts to construct a shrine for Kalliamman on the border of Udayallipatti main village and has been collecting money from politicians, officials, farmers, his own castemen and others. However, regarding the collection one of his castemen complained to the researcher that SBS is forcing each family to pay Rs.300 which they can not afford. It was reported later that he has successfully completed the construction of the shrine.

SBS does not have any political affiliation in particular. He contested as an independent candidate in Kulathur (Reserved) constituency in the Assembly elections in 1984. He polled only 1011 votes while the AIADMK (Jayalalitha) candidate V. Raju won with 47,624 votes in that election.

Interestingly, his elder son is an engineer, the only professional job holder in the village. When questioned as to who from the village is the most educated youth and gone out for a job to any respondent, the immediate answer is pointing out to SBS's elder son. Sometimes followed by the comment only they (meaning

SCs') are getting educated.

PROFILES OF POWER HOLDERS : A COMPARATIVE ANALYSIS

The above are the profiles of power holders who control one or more sources of power. An attempt is made below to compare and analyse the socio-economic background of different power holders and their sources of powers.

Socio-economic factors considered include caste, age, education, occupation, landholding and positions held-formal or informal or both. Further, power holders are classified on the basis of their position in the local caste and social hierarchy. The classification of caste and social hierarchy places cultivators like Kallars and Udayars on the high position. Asaris, Vannars and Navithars, service castes in the middle and Pusaris and SCs who are by and large agricultural labourers in the lower position. On the basis of above classification the data is presented in Table 5.1.

The table 5.1 suggests that most of the power holders are from Kallar caste and it seems caste plays an important role as a source of power. As it was described in the profiles, among Kallars, persons from Mangalar clan have come to occupy important positions both formal and informal in the Udayallipatti Panchayat. It may be recollected that the Kallars constitute the largest single caste group in the Panchayat. Among Kallars, Mangalars are largest in number and they hold more lands than any other title holders among Kallars. As far as age is concerned, most of them are above 50 years and are educated upto primary level.

Irrespective of social and caste position, almost all the power holders are cultivators. However, landownership of the power holders presents a mixed picture of a minimum of four to twenty seven acres. It was shown in the earlier chapters that Udayars are better placed in terms of land ownership than Kallars. The large landowners are from Udayar caste. However they have not held any formal position. None of them is a prominent leader of the village. Most of the formal and informal positions have been held by Kallars.

To analyse the power holders further, let us turn to see who has what source or sources of power. The table 5.2. presents the cumulative data on various power holders having different sources of power. (see graph 5.1.)

Table 5.1 : Socio-Economic Background of Power Holders

Power holder	Caste (Age)	Education	Occupation	Land-holding (acres)	Formal or informal position or both
Upper Caste					
HM	Kallar (57)	Primary	Cultivator	20	Caste and Village leader-Panchayat President
QM	Kallar (50)	Primary	Cultivator	10	Caste and village leader-Panchayat President.
TM	Kallar (45)	Higher	Cultivator	15	Caste and village leader-AIADMK Union Secretary
WMR	Kallar	Higher	Cultivator	10	Presidents, Milk & Sheep Breeders Co-operatives
SP	Kallar (61)	Primary	Cultivator	09	President, Primary A-Credit Society
BM	Kallar (68)	Illiterate	Cultivator	15	Caste leader
PNM	Kallar (75)	Primary	Cultivator	07	Caste and village leader.
KSU	Udayar (40)	Primary	Cultivator	27	Big landowner
IPU	Udayar (60)	Illiterate	Cultivator	20	Big landowner
Middle Caste					
KMA	Christian Asari (50)	Illiterate	Blacksmith	06	Vice-President of Panchayat
Lower Caste					
PHP	Pusari (40)	Primary	Cultivator	10	Caste leader-DMK Party Cadre
SBS	SC (57)	Illiterate	Cultivator	04	Caste leader

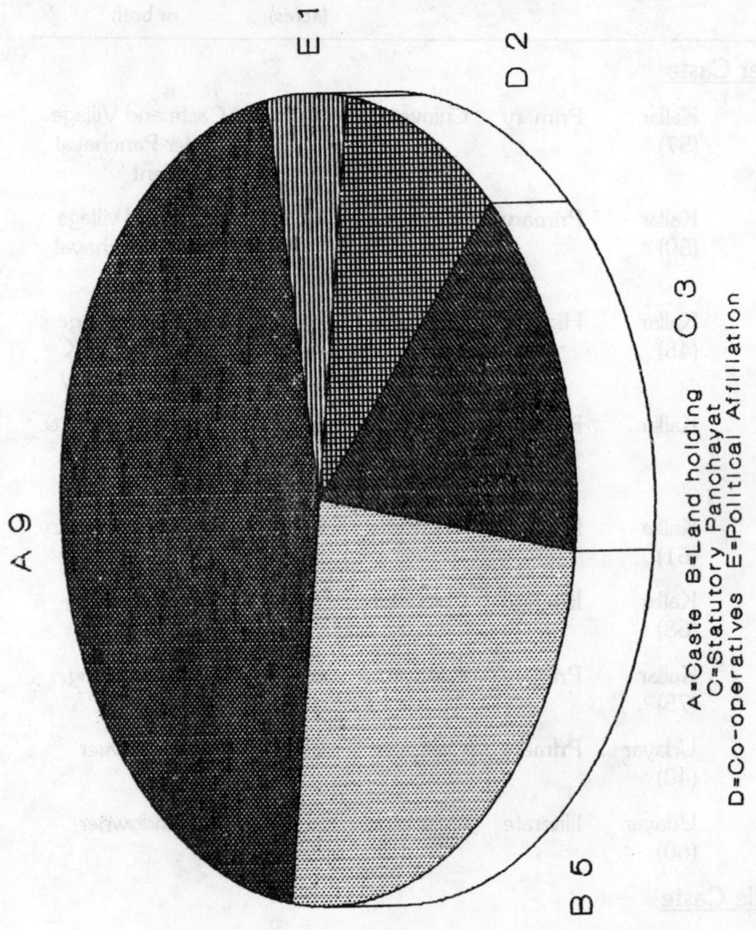

Graph 5.1: Power Holders and their Sources of Power

It must be emphasised here that since the study is of historical nature, the data should be interpreted not as a situation at a particular point of time but keeping in mind continuity and changes. Hence, the classification attempted is here for analytical purpose only.

Table 5.2 : Power holders and Their Sources of Power

Power Holder	Caste	Land-Holding	Statutory Panchayat	Co-operatives	Political Affiliation
Upper Caste					
HM	*	*	*	—	—
QM	*	—	*	—	—
TM	*	—	—	—	*
WMR	*	—	—	*	—
SP	*	—	—	*	—
BM	*	—	—	—	—
PNM	*	—	—	—	—
KSU	—	*	—	—	—
TPU	—	*	—	—	—
Middle caste					
KMA	—	—	*	—	—
Lower caste					
PHP	*	*	—	—	DMK cadre for two decades
SBS	*	—	—	—	Lost as an independent MLA in the 1984 Assembly elections

* Source of power

The table 5.2 suggests that most of the power holders have caste as a source of power and those who have caste as a source of power also have other sources of power. Kallars constitute the largest number of power holders with caste as a basis of power.

As for as landholding is concerned as was discussed earlier, big landowners are more in number in Udayar caste than in Kallar caste. The table suggests that among the Udayars, two persons are relatively bigger landowners though neither of them is a caste leader nor hold any formal or informal position. However, this does not undermine the importance of land as a source of power. Among the power holders from Kallars HM and TM have had formal position and have become big landowners after being in office.

The statutory Panchayat provides two Kallars and one Asari basis for power. These two Kallars are from Mangalar clan. The President of Co-operatives, on the other hand, were not from Mangalar clan though from Kallar caste. The reason might be the territorial demarcation of Co-operatives are different from Panchayat boundary.

In the profile of various power holders, details are given about political affiliations of different persons. However, as the above table suggests only one person from Kallar caste held a party post and another person from Pusari caste has been DMK cadre for many years. Another person contested as an independent in the Assembly elections in 1984 and lost. Most others do have political affiliation but not to the extent of any formal positions bringing power to the persons.

In the beginning of this chapter it was proposed to classify power holders in terms of possession of internal or external or both sources of power. Accordingly, out of twelve power holders six have internal sources like caste or landholding as a sources of power and only one person has exclusively external source of power. Rest of them have both external sources like statutory Panchayat, Co-operatives and political affiliation as well as internal sources like caste and landholding.

SUMMING-UP

This chapter, thus, focused on the power holders and their sources of power. An attempt has also been made on the basis of these profiles to compare the socio-economic background of power holders. It was found that most of them come from upper caste. Among upper caste Kallars have come to occupy important positions. However, biggest landowners are not Kallars but Udayars. In terms of occupation most of them are cultivators. Further most of them are above fifty years and are educated up to primary level.

In terms of sources most of them have caste as a source of power and next comes land as a source. Almost all the positions in the formal institutions which include statutory Village Panchayat, Co-operatives and political parties have been held by Kallars. While half of the power holders have exclusively internal source of power and the other half, except for one person, possess both external and internal sources.

The analysis presented in this chapter, as mentioned earlier, should not be viewed as if it is the situation obtained at a particular point of time. There have been changes affecting different sources which in turn affect power holders. Hence, the next chapter focuses on the inter-relationship between sources of power and power holders.

NOTES AND REFERENCES

1. Pseudonyms are used to maintain the confidentiality of the information.
2. Barbarra Harriss, *Child Nutrition and Poverty in South India* (New Delhi : Concept, 1991), pp.69-70.
3. The details of this case study is given in chapter-VI.
4. The researcher has witnessed many times when SB was called even by upper caste persons as SB swamy.

Transformation of Power

In the previous chapters the discussion focused on how various sources of power have given rise to different power holders, their socio-economic background and their respective sources of power. This chapter focuses on the inter-relationship between sources of power and power holders in the study area in terms of continuities and changes in the sources of power and its impact on the power holders.

Before analysing the inter-relating factors, it would be helpful to draw certain broad contours of sources of power and power holders during Pre-Independence period. This would also be helpful to understand continuities and changes which might have occurred after independence in the power formation. It must be emphasised here that this serves only limited purpose of a broader understanding of power formation before independence as the data collected may not be totally accurate because either records are not available or the memories of informants are dim and they tend to exaggerate their past.

During the rule of Thondaiman Kings in the 1920s and 30s, local authority stemmed from two sources. One was based on landholding and another belonging to royal caste that is Kallar caste. These two were recognised by the state and the authority was given at local level to maintain law and order in the village and to collect taxes. As Dirks informs us that these two authorities are mostly the same as persons from Kallar caste were also conferred Miraci rights to collect taxes. These two positions were called 'Miracidars' and 'Ambalars'.[1]

In the main village, however, two Udayars were recognised as Miracidars and conferred Miraci rights. Miracidars were to collect revenue for the state and acted as a government agent for all village concerns.[2] Subsequently the posts of 'Maniam' and 'Karnam' were introduced supplementing the role of Miracidars. In the adjoining areas of Udayallipatti Panchayat Kallars were conferred with Miraci rights and they were also Ambalars.[3] The role of Miracidars gradually declined as their functions were taken over by Maniam and Karnam who were usually local men. They were replaced in 1982 by Village Administrative Officers (VAO), thereby cutting off local element in the revenue collection process.[4]

Before independence Ambalar acted as a link between the local level and the King. He maintained order in the village and acted as an adjudicator along with the village elders. This position was usually given to one of the three 'Karai' Mangalars in the main village. By virtue of his position, Ambalar was given 'prasadam' first in the Veerapondor Koil during festivals. In the main village AM was the Ambalar and his son, QM was the Panchayat President for a term starting from 1986. AM was a big landowner and his son continued to hold his lands though not to the extent his father owned. His family is still referred to as Ambalar family. Introduction of Panchayati Raj system in Tamil Nadu made the formal authority of Ambalar redundant. AM was a consensus President for a few years. When the local Kallar groups wanted an election for the position in 1958 he withdrew from the contest.

Apart from these, power holders comprised of big landowners like, MK Udayar, Duraiswamy Mangalar, Palaniappa Chettiar, Babar Khan Saybu, and a few other Kallars and Udayars. According to some elderly respondents only when all of them joined together consensus could be reached on any issues pertaining to the village. A common element of these men was that all of them were big landowners. In fact, MK Udayar was the biggest landowner in the village owning a separate irrigation tank. Palaniappa Chettiar was owner of most of the present Kallar lands as evident from the land records of 1960.

After independence, however, changes have taken place in the power formation because of introduction of universal adult franchise and institutions like village Panchayats and various Co-operatives. These institutions have emerged as new sources of power unlike earlier situation where landholding and social ranking constituted as sources of power. Apart from these caste system seems to be undergoing changes which in turn affecting power formation. Political parties are also playing their role thereby making an impact on the local power formation. For the purpose of understanding the changes in the sources of power and their impact on power holders, the foregoing analysis is attempted.

1) CASTE STRUCTURE AND POWER FORMATION

This section inquires into the linkages between caste and political power. In other words, how and why some persons have come to acquire political - formal and informal - power on the basis of caste. Is it because of numerical dominance of one or more caste or kinship network or the very arrangement of stratified inter-caste relationship or is it a combination of different factors ?

Firstly, let us take note of numerical dominance. To recollect briefly the points made earlier that the Kallar caste is the largest single group with 37 percent of votes. Hypothetically speaking other major caste groups which include Udayars(16 percent), Konars (10 percent), Pusaris(9 percent) SCs(8 percent) Asaris (7 percent) and Gounders (6 percent) with the combined strength of 56 percent would have ensured a candidate from other than Kallar caste to get elected in a contest between a Kallar and a non-Kallar candidate in the Panchayat elections conducted in 1986. However, only two Kallars, contested as it had been always since 1958. Even a multi-cornered contest would have ensured a win for other caste candidate as it happened in 1986 Panchayat elections in Killukottai Panchayat.

It was stated earlier that Kallars with varying strength in 38 Panchayats have come to occupy most of the posts of Panchayat President and Panchayat Union Chairmen. Further, in the Panchayat as well as in a few surrounding Panchayats among Kallars the clan claiming original settlers status have come to occupy the President post. In the case of the Udayallipatti Panchayat, it was Mangalars who claim original settlers status. Now the question is how Kallars, particularly Mangalars could be able to acquire and retain formal political power despite not having an absolute majority of their own in terms of voters. There are two aspects to be considered in this situation. Firstly, why the other caste voters supported Kallars, assuming each caste member votes for his/her own caste candidate including Kallars in a situation of multi-cornered contest. Closely related to the first dimension is the of second one where Kallars claim traditional political authority in local politics either in terms of 'Ur' Panchayat or temple activities.

To take the dimension of voters support to Kallar candidates. Firstly, it is to be noted that in the 1986 Panchayat elections the voters had no choice except to vote for one Kallar candidate or the other. It is hypothetical to talk about a multi-cornered contest where, as shown earlier, other castes with their combined strength might have made a non-Kallar candidate to win the elections. However, still what could be the main considerations for voting for Kallar candidates? One Asari respondent, though known as supporter of QM felt :

" HM has been successful for three terms because he is a capable man and could get things done for the village and is also clever in managing the Panchayat affairs".

However, a Kallar respondent, a former President of the Primary Agriculture Co-operative Society perceived it in a different way:"It is not the question of ability to do good or bad work. People vote on the basis of 'vendiapattall'.

"What do you mean by vendiapattall"?

"It means that a particular candidate is closer to me in terms of relationship like cousin (Pangali) or uncle or nephew or he has done me some favours or he is likely to do me favours".

Respondents from other castes as well reacted in a similar way. Thus, the past performance and relationship a voter has with the candidate broadly determines the choice of the candidates for voting.

Questioned as to why nobody other than Kallar candidates contested in the 1986 Panchayat elections as it happened in the adjacent Killukottai Panchayat, the typical response was that Kallars will not allow others to contest and others are afraid of

Kallars. When enquired as to why Udayars who are economically and socially equal to Kallars did not bid for power, one young Udayar respondent replied.

"We don't have unity among ourselves to put up our candidate. Further, we are not sure of getting votes from people belonging to other castes like Pusaris, Konars Gounders and SCs as they are traditional supporters of Kallars and in case of disputes they approach Kallars not us".

Udayars are not in the forefront in the village politics both in 'Ur' panchayat and in the common village affairs like temple festivals. Respondents frequently stated "they generally mind their business of cultivation". These might be the reasons for Udayars not challenging Kallar candidates. As to the other castes - Pusaris and SCs do not have sufficient numerical strength to put up their own candidate. Further, they neither came together nor was there any other upper caste candidate except Kallars contesting the elections in 1986 as it happened in Killukottai.

Why do only Mangalars among the Kallars contest the Panchayat elections, not to speak of getting elected to the position ? One young Kallar respondent's answer was typical :

"Mangalars will not allow Kallars from other clans to contest because they would say 'you belong to Poonadi kannikai' (persons who were married into Mangalar clan from outside and settled in the village) and we (Mangalars) have been here originally for long'. And, people from other clans are related to Mangalars as uncles, nephews etc. Hence, others would hesitate to antagonise the Mangalars"

Though members of other clans have not contested in the Panchayat elections for the post of President some section of Kallars like Palandors are known in the village to take side generally with kilkarai Mangalar, BM, who was opposed to HM in the 1958 Panchayat elections. Recently, in the 1986 Panchayat elections they supported QM. And so Mangalar dominance over other Kallar clans is not decisive and there has been competition for power among Mangalars. Factionalism prevailing for many years among these groups has extended to the Panchayat elections also.

Thus, it can be inferred that the reasons such as Kallars being the largest single group and the absence of multi-cornered contest are not sufficient to explain their capacity to capture formal positions. To add to these are the social and economic position of Kallars in the village, dominance in 'Ur'panchayat and their role in temple activities.

As noted earlier, Kallars, along with Udayars, Konars etc. who are mainly cultivators are placed in the local level on the top of the caste hierarchy. Servicing castes like Asaris, Vannars etc., and Pusaris and SCs mainly agricultural labourers are placed below Kallars. The social positions of different castes, by and large, are in congruence with their economic positions. The lower castes are still dependent on cultivators for their subsistence, at least during the peak seasons. The cultivators like Udayars and Kallars possess, as it was shown in the previous chapter, most of the lands in the village. This gives Kallars and Udayars power over other castes as others are dependent on them for employment.

Udayars are also placed socially and economically more or less on the same level with Kallars. However, they seem to have been playing subordinate role to Kallars. Not that the dominance of Kallars has never been challenged by Udayars. Under the leadership of MK Udayar 40 years back Udayars challenged Kallars over the right of sacrificing goat first in the Veerapondor temple. This resulted in a clash between Udayars and Kallars. The matter was settled in favour of Kallars with the intervention of local police. The agreement made was that Kallars would give the sacrifice first and then Udayars. This practice continues even today.

Recalling the incident, an elderly Udayar commented "After MK Udayar, no leader has emerged in our caste to challenge Kallars". The dominance of Kallars, apart from day to day behaviour is more evident in their dominance in 'Ur' panchayat activities. Other castes are tied to Kallars in a patron-client relationship as was shown in an earlier chapter. This is as well true of Udayars who approach Kallars for solving even intra-caste disputes, though they are socially and economically equal to Kallars.

There were many disputes where Kallars have intervened and settled them. In the recent years, Kallar leaders like QM and PNM intervened in a family quarrel between Asari families. Another dispute among Pusaris which even led to police complaint was eventually resolved by QM and PNM.

During the course of the fieldwork a dispute involving a boy and a girl from two communities got the village assembled to witness the panchayat. This was important because 'Ur' panchayat was not conducted for many years since the theft of 'Murugan idol' from Veerapondor Koil which resulted in two factions of Kallars accusing each other of theft. The details of the dispute are as follows.

"A Muslim boy, son of a petty shop owner in the main village, was accused of misbehaving with a girl from one of the service castes. This matter was brought to the notice of QM, HM and PNM. In turn they agreed to call for 'Ur' panchayat. In the panchayat both parties were called to give their version. From the girl's side they could present the case convincingly in the panchayat and they also brought out some evidences of boy's misbehaviour not only in this case but also on other occasions. Though the boy denied the charges initially, however, he accepted them subsequently. The panchayat decided to fine him and instead of the panchayat specifying an amount as fine they made the boy to pick it himself from among several slips specifying amount ranging from Rs 200 to 700. The boy chose a paper which mentioned Rs.700/- and accordingly he was asked to pay the amount towards temple funds".

This case demonstrates that Kallars, despite problems among themselves over Murugan idol theft, could call for 'Ur' panchayat and people from other caste also respond to the call. So also Kallars could enforce their decision on disputing parties thereby ensuring their power over other castes.

The dominance of Kallars in internal politics also reflects in the religious activities of the village like organising festivals in various temples and shrines particularly for the Veerapondor Koil where Kallars take the lead. During the festivals, the Ambalar is given 'prasadam' followed by others.[5] HM was the trustee of the temple earlier and at present his brother TM a former Panchayat Union Secretary for AIADMK holds the post.

Thus, Kallars play a prominent role in the religious activities of the village. Though the phenomenon of people from different castes visiting temples in Palani and Sabarimalai is spreading in the area its impact on the dominance of Kallars in the religious activity at local level is not clearly evident. However, it might be interpreted that by conducting the festivals regularly symbolic assertion of

Kallars over the local society is ensured. According to Harriss, the main village festivals appear to express solidarity of the village but they also reinforce hierarchy.[6]

In the recent years, however, the dispute within two sections of Kallars over Murugan idol theft in Veerapondor temple lead to near break down of the dominance of Kallars over the religious activities and it even affected the unity of Kallars. Thus, this dispute deserves elaboration.

In 1982, the 'Murugan' idol was stolen from the Veerapondor temple. Being the trustee TM lodged a complaint in the local police station and mentioning a few names of Mangalars and Palandors as suspects. This led to the arrest of these persons. All of them denied involvement in the theft and were later released on bail. The affected section of Kallars felt that they were wrongly implicated in the theft and from then on they refused to participate in the temple activities. Hence, festivals could not be conducted regularly. When it was conducted the accused section did not participate in the festivals. This went on for sometime until PNM,a Kallar leader (see profile of power holders) made efforts to bring two sections together. It took him almost two years to accomplish the task, as disputing factions did not want to come to a compromise. However, only in 1990 he was able to make both sections of Kallars to participate in the festival of the Veerapondor temple on the understanding that since the crime is not proved and there is no use fighting among Kallars and this would undermine their standing in the village community. Finally PNM could conduct the festival for the Veerapondor temple with all the sections of Kallars who were involved in the dispute.

The above dispute among Kallars indicates that they get united when it comes to common village matters to assert their dominance. This also confirms the assertion of various respondents that Kallars, despite factions among them, get united whenever it is necessary.

What ensures the dominance of Kallars in the local politics? There appears to be many factors responsible for this. The total landholding and higher social ranking of the Kallar caste are not sufficient grounds for political dominance as Udayars are also placed in more or less the same position. Apart from landholding and social ranking it is their internal unity whenever a threat comes from other castes and 'tradition' of threat of violence or violence itself by Kallars ensuring their claim to local political power.

In this context, when PNM, who successfully mediated the dispute over Murugan idol theft and also many more disputes for the past thirty years, was asked as how it is possible for Kallars to dominate local politics. He said:

> *"It is all because of strength of numbers and unity of Kallars. Further, in case some do not obey our decision or not willing to come to 'Ur' panchayat we create some hurdles so that they fall in line".*

This has been the general response of the many respondents which include Kallars and other caste people. Despite a sense of unity or cohesion of caste within Kallars there have been factional fights. An elderly informant recollected that there have always been two factions in the village one led by middle karai Mangalars and another by upper karai Mangalars. The middle karai led by HM and his brother TM, and the upper karai led by QM and some Palandors. From the lower karai some families like that of BM have been supporting QM. PNM who belongs to lower karai is a traditional supporter of HM but shifted his support as noted in his profile from HM to QM before the 1986 Panchayat elections. There have been many factional fights even in the recent years involving HM & TM on the one hand and QM on the other. However, one factional fight needs to be mentioned here because it involved all the three karai Mangalars and some section of other clan Kallars and centred around PNM and his shift of support from HM to QM.

Immediately after the defeat of HM in the 1986 Panchayat elections on one occasion he shouted at PNM for having shifted his support though he has taken care of PNM in terms of food and clothing. On hearing this, some youth from Palandor clan who were all along opposed HM and his brother TM informed him through the third party that PNM was their man now and HM should not abuse him. If he continued like this he would get beaten up.

Next day some youth of Palandor and lower karai Mangalars went to the house of HM threatening to beat him. However, it was prevented by some Kallars. Further, at that time neither HM or TM was there in their houses. On the following day, a Palandor youth walked before HMs house several times. This infuriated HMs first son who was watching the moments of the Palandor youth all along. He shouted at the Palandor youth and accused him of working as PNM's spy. This resulted in exchange of words and in the process HM's first son slapped the Palandor youth. Interestingly, this news was reported to both HM and TM who were in their fields as if HM's son was beaten up. Immediately HM and TM along with their brothers and relatives rushed with knife and sticks. They reached the houses of Palandors where PNM was staying and challenged Palandors and PNM to come out and fight. However, as there was no response from the other side the HM's group withdrew after they were pacified by other Kallars.

This dispute shows the existence of factionalism among the Kallars. However, the resolution of Murugon idol theft case in 1990 demonstrates that though there have been factional fights mostly between three karai Kallars they can unite at times of need. Not that all the factional problems are solved. At least for the time being they get subsumed. It was later reported to the researcher that in the festival conducted in 1990, PNM, QM, and TM aligned themselves while HM was isolated. This was because of the differences that have developed between HM and his brother TM over the dispute between a Udayar and TM (mentioned elsewhere earlier) wherein HM supported the Udayar and not his brother.

Thus, though there have been factional fights among the Kallars there is a tendency to show caste unity regarding inter-caste disputes or matters concerning village common interest. Further, there is a general fear of Kallars among other castes as something would happen if one does not listen to the Kallars. This fear does not seem to exist without foundation as Kallars have proved by way of cattle lifting etc.[7] Added to these factors, are the presence of Kallars in the surrounding villages and their strong kinship network and the tradition of 'Ur'panchayats between villages mediated mainly by Kallar leaders. Though Pusaris and SCs are also widespread in the taluk they are socially and economically not in a stronger position compared to Kallars.

If other castes like Pusaris, SCs, Konars and Gounders are playing sub-ordinate role what about Udayars? Both in electoral or in local politics they are playing sub-ordinate role despite larger landholding and higher social ranking. Earlier, MK Udayar with his larger landholding and as a Karnam played a dominant role in the village. Now the Udayars despite having better land-man ratio and with larger number of big landowners are not in a position to assert themselves in the local politics. In fact, the Udayars themselves are divided supporting one section of the Kallars or the others. It can be interpreted that the Kallars are successful in dividing the Udayars. It may also be interpreted that it is other way round i.e., by supporting one section of Kallars in the elections or in the local disputes, the Udayars are making sure that the Kallars are not united. In that case, each section of Kallars would seek the support of different Udayars which leaves the options for Udayars to play one against the other.[8]

To sum up, Kallars - the largest single group could be able to win and retain formal positions in the village so far. Despite other groups combined constitute more than Kallars fail to capture these formal positions and Kallars particularly Mangalars,could gather votes from other castes. The occupation of Kallars in formal positions might be linked to their dominance in local politics and temple activities. Kallars not only show solidarity among themselves in times of need but also could be in a position to divide other castes in various matters. Other castes are dependent on Kallars for solving their disputes. Even Udayars who are socially and economically on par with Kallars also approach Kallars for solving the disputes. Kallars could exercise their dominance because of their demonstration of unity despite factional fights and their tradition of threat of violence in some cases violence itself.

Now the question is whether political dominance of Kallars particularly of Mangalars decisive in the village. It does not seem so at least since the late eighties. There are evidences to show that domination of Kallars is being challenged now which will be the subject of discussion at later stage of this chapter.

2) LANDHOLDING AND POWER FORMATION

It has been noted that in 1960 total lands of the Udayars was more than that of Kallars. However in 1990, the Kallars had an edge over the Udayars in terms of total lands. Despite this the Udayars have a more favourable land-man ratio than the Kallars. Thus, it can be concluded broadly as on 1990 both the Kallars and Udayars are economically dominant over the other castes in the revenue village. Further, while the total lands of Brahmins, Muslims and Chettiars have decreased, the total land of Pusaris, Gounders and Konars have increased in 1990 when compared with the 1960 figures.

Though it has been possible with the help of land records to identify changes in the landholdings among different castes but difficult to account for all the factors responsible for these changes[9] However, some explanation can be attempted on the basis of information provided by the respondents.

The Kallars have acquired lands mainly from Chettiars and Brahmins and more so from the former. They were working as tenants for Chettiar landowners. When the Chettiar families were selling their lands mostly Kallars - their former tenants - bought these lands. Some Kallar respondents claimed that originally these lands were their ancestral property which the Chettiars appropriated through the process of money lending. Even some Udayars bought lands from the Chettiar families.

Another way the Kallars seem to have acquired lands over a period of time is through creating a situation whereby other caste people would sell their lands. In a recent dispute between two brothers from scheduled caste it was reported that a Kallar was responsible for inciting the same. This led the brothers to go to police and subsequently to court which involved spending money. It was reported later that one of the brothers wanted to sell his lands to meet his court expenses and the same Kallar was reportedly planning to buy them.

There is another case pending in the court involving a prominent Kallar leader and a Udayar backed by the Kallar's brother. The former entered into an agreement to cultivate the lands of the latter for a particular period. Once the period was over the Kallar refused to hand over the lands to the Udayar arguing that he incurred debts in improving the lands and deepening the well and Udayar had to pay for these debts before claiming back the lands. Udayar refused to accept this proposal and the matter was taken to court at the instance of the Kallar's brother. Though his brother argued with the Kallar leader in favour of the Udayar he has refused to handover the lands. While the case is pending in the court the Kallar continued to cultivate the land.

Though these case studies themselves are not sufficient to understand the changes in land transactions over the years yet they partly reveal the process and there may be economic factors responsible for their changes.

Another aspect of landholding is the relationship between political power and economic power. In other words, is land a source of political power? Forty years back politically important persons in Udayallipatti were big landowners. Earlier some owned more than fifty acres and now big landowners own only twenty five acres or so. The distribution of lands now is much more diffused now than it was earlier. There is a large number of small landowners even in the politically dominant Kallar caste.

Results of the enquiry into landholdings of different political leaders reveal some trends. To take the case of HM and TM both were small landowners at the beginning of their political career and have come to possess more than 15 acres now. There are other leaders like QM who had large amount of lands now selling his lands off gradually, though his father was one of the big landowners. PNM another Kallar leader had more lands in the village but now sold them off and settled down in the nearby town. PHP, a longstanding DMK activist, possesses more than fifteen acres of lands. Most of the big landowners now belong to Udayar caste though politically they have been playing sub-ordinate role to Kallars at the local level. It is to be noted that none of the Udayars have held any formal position since MK Udayar. He held a large area of land and a seperate tank. As noted earlier he was a Karnam and the only Udayar to ever hold any formal position after independence from the village.

Thus, though Kallars have to share the economic dominance with the Udayars, they have increased their land holding considerably compared to Udayars over the years. Among Kallars some political leaders seem to have acquired economic power through their official position.

3) INSTITUTIONS, PARTY POLITICS AND POWER FORMATION

It is better to analyse both institutions and party politics together as they provide a linkage between local level and outside and also there seems to be a link between these two things. To sum up the points made earlier - the persons from Kallar caste have come to occupy important political positions either in Panchayats or Co-operatives as Presidents or in political parties. Despite Kallars occupying important political positions there appears to be changes at different points of time in the relative political power of the various leaders as a result of linkage between institutions and party politics.

In the case of Panchayat there was a gap of sixteen years in conducting elections to these bodies. Hence, it severed a formal political link between the local level and the government all these years. Even when elections were conducted in 1986 by the AIADMK government the Village Panchayats were stripped off most of the powers.[10] During these interim period another type of linkage seems to have emerged, that is party leaders acting as intermediaries between the local level and the government. For instance, the emergence of TM as a political leader is the result of his mediation between local people and the government.

On the other hand, the role of HM, as a middleman has declined for two reasons. Firstly, he was not President for sixteen years there by reducing his influence as a middleman. Secondly, he lost the 1986 Panchayat elections thereby losing his institutional authority. Another President QM seems mainly to have won on negative votes against HM. His performance has been dismal compared to HM. His term saw Panchayat without much powers though some powers were delegated by the DMK government. The only power he has enjoyed was to get contracts and that too on one occasion he had given the contract to a prominent scheduled caste leader.

There is another leader emerging in the recent years on the basis of formal position in co-operative societies viz., WMR from Alwanpatti. His powers are also limited by the election not being conducted regularly to these bodies and they have, unlike Panchayats, limited franchise restricted to eligible members. He seems to be another emerging centre of power sometimes challenging other Kallar leaders from the main village. This was evident from the co-operative elections in 1990 where Kallar leaders from Udayallipatti opposed him through Konars from Alwanpatti.

In the late seventies and eighties there was the absence of formal and effective links through statutory Village Panchayats partly because there was a gap of many years in conducting the elections to these bodies in Tamil Nadu, and partly also because even after the elections conducted in 1986 they were left without much powers. This situation has made political linkage through political parties to play a greater role between the local and the higher levels. This was evident from the rise of TM as a political leader whose influence as a middleman extends upto the state level. It was shown earlier as to how he has acquired arrack shop contracts through his political links and has also got jobs for some young men. On one occasion he has used his political links with R M Veerappan, then a minister in MGR government, to bail him out of arrest by the local police over a quarrel with other Kallars. In the late eighties he seems to have lost his political power in a series of miscalculated moves whereby he aligned with parties which did not come to power in the 1989 and 1991 Assembly elections.

A noted feature of these power holders is their external linkage. Apart from internal bases, their sources of power have external linkages. As far as Village Panchayat and Co-operatives are concerned their links with the various officials of government departments provide them with necessary resources for distributing patronage to their clients and also it provides them opportunities for gaining wealth. Political parties provide another external linkage to persons holding positions in the party. In the village Union secretary of AIADMK did make use of his political connections as evident from his getting jobs for some young men, permission for many arrack shops, use of political connection when he was arrested by the police and so on to enhance his position in the area.

To sum up, the role of power holders with formal institutions as the sources of power in the village has declined in the seventies and eighties. This is because of irregular conduct of elections and lack of powers to these bodies. However, power holders, on the other hand, with position in political parties have emerged to act as mediators between the local and higher levels.

4) 'DOMINANT PERSONS' WITHIN DOMINANT CASTE

The preceding analysis focused on inter-relationship between the sources of power and power holders highlighting that there are some persons who are dominant within Kallar caste which has most of the elements of a dominant caste as propounded by Srinivas.[11] Before analysing the dominant persons within dominant caste it is necessary to compare the findings in the Udayallipatti Panchayat with the concept of dominant caste and also to find out whether any caste is decisively dominant. This is necessary because this concept has been discussed extensively in the social sciences to understand and comment upon the phenomenon of power in the rural areas.

The concept of dominant caste as first used by Srinivas meant that a caste may be said to be dominant when it preponderates numerically over other castes and when it also wields preponderant economic and political power. A large and powerful caste group can be more easily dominant if its position in the local caste hierarchy is not too low.[12] Later another criterion of dominance that is, of western education and occupations was added. Further, Srinivas feels that "usually different elements of dominance are distributed among different castes in a village. If a caste enjoys all or most of the elements of dominance it may be said to have decisive dominance".[13]

The concept of dominant caste, however, has been subjected to criticism on many grounds by different authors particularly Dumont,[14] Dube [15] and Oommen.[16] However, the application of the concept in the Udayallipatti Panchayat shows that the Kallar caste possesses most of the elements of dominance except that only very few persons are in the professional jobs.

As far as numerical strength is concerned the Kallars are the largest single group who could prevent others from even contesting the Panchayat elections.Thus, numerical strength of Kallars is useful when they could be able to get votes from other castes also. Numerical strength may not be a sufficient ground for their dominance in local politics and also their unity is important and is contextual. According to Srinivas, it emerges especially in relation to opposition to other castes.[17] The dominance of Kallars in 'Ur' panchayat is linked with their claim of traditional political authority in terms of original settlers, Ambalar as headman and his importance in temple activities.

Though Kallars on the whole owned more lands in 1990 compared to 1960, they have to share the economic power over other castes with Udayars. Kallars also share the same social status with Udayars, Konars and Gounders though politically they are not dominant as they also approach Kallars for resolving inter-caste and intra-caste matters. They also play a sub-ordinate role in 'Ur' panchayats and in temple festivals.

Dube challenges the concept of dominant caste by stating that a number of dominant individuals occupying most of the power positions belong to a particular caste by itself is not enough to characterise a caste as dominant. However, he concedes the existence of dominant individuals within dominant caste.[18] Reacting to this criticism, Srinivas[19] concedes that there are dominant individuals within dominant caste. Nonetheless,he adds that dominant individuals "owe their dominance to the fact that they are a part of the dominant caste." It is true of Udayallipatti Panchayat that there are dominant individuals within dominant caste, viz., Kallar caste. Interestingly among different Kallar clans, Mangalar clan occupies most of the formal and informal positions in the Panchayat village. In the village Panchayat Kallars from Mangalar clan so far occupied several positions. The members of Mangalar clan also take active part in Ur panchayat and in temple activities. The person from the same clan was an important functionary in AIADMK party. Hence, the concept of dominant caste has to take into considerations not only different elements of dominance but also the existence of dominant persons within dominant caste. In this context the study agrees with the view that the dominant caste as a whole is an arena within which particular lineages exert superior power.

5) FACTIONALISM AND POWER FORMATION

Another aspect of the concept of dominant caste which is under challenge is that of existence of factionalism within dominant caste. Dube[20] challenges that the notion of dominant caste is untenable unless the unity of the caste as a group is assumed. Srinivas[21] also recognises that endemic factionalism is a threat to the continued existence of a dominant caste. According to Oommen[22] there exist a high degree of factionalism in Indian villages, and more often than not, it is the numerically superior and/or economically well-off castes which are sharply divided into conflicting power groups. Dumont concedes that among the members of dominant caste there would be rivalries or factions once they are numerous.[23]

The situation as obtained from Udayallipatti shows the existence of factionalism for many years among Kallars. According to elderly respondents the village witnessed mainly two factions.

Mention has already been made in the previous chapters about the existence of these factions -one led by HM and supported by middle Karai Mangalars and another led by QM and supported by kilkarai Mangalars and Palandors. There has been, however, shift ot members from one faction to another. For instance withdrawing of support by PNM to HM with whom he had long association. PNM was responsible to put forward the candidature of HM in the 1958 Panchayat elections. The shift of support by PNM from HM to QM in the 1986 Panchayat elections has resulted in the factional fight between these two factions. Another factional fight in recent years happened over Murugan idol theft case which almost destroyed the unity of Kallars for many years. In this case also both the factions were involved. There have been other factional fights involving both these factions.

Now the question is how far the existence of factionalism in the dominant caste threatens the unity which is essential for its continuing dominance ? Dube[24] asserts that the existence of unity within dominant caste is essential for its dominance. For Srinivas, the unity of a caste, particularly that of a dominant caste, is not something static and constant, but dynamic and contextual. It emerges in a relation of opposition to the other caste.[25]

As far as Udayallipatti Panchayat is concerned, though there have been factional fights among Kallars they have demonstrated unity so far. This is evident from the way all the factions of Kallars attended the 'Ur' panchayat called to dispense justice in a case involving persons from two communities other than Kallars. Subsequently this paved the way for resolution of conflict between two factions over Murugan idol theft case and conducting of the festivals for Veerapondor Koil with all the sections of Kallars participating in it. Despite this situation there are trends emerging which might challenge the dominance of Kallars and particularly Mangalar clan.

6) EMERGING TRENDS

This section is not intended to deal exhaustively with the emerging trends in the power formation. However based on the above analysis and discussions with some respondents a brief account of emerging trends is presented.

It was mentioned earlier that there are indications to show that the political dominance of Mangalars, if not Kallars as whole, is being challenged since the late eighties. One indication being Murugan idol theft case resulting in division of Kallars which took almost eight years to resolve. Though factional fights were common earlier as well, the theft case indicates that the internal unity of Kallars is fragile now and Mangalars' hold over other Kallars seems to be under challenge.

Further, when an young Kallar respondent was questioned about the possible emerging situation in the Panchayat village, he responded that in the Panchayat elections to be held in the future some section of Kallar youths have decided to put up a candidate not necessarily from Mangalar clan. He also felt that there may be candidates likely to contest from Alwanpatti. This situation has arisen, according to him, for two reasons. Firstly, among Kallars, particularly between TM and HM, there have been more quarrels in recent times some times leading to court cases. Secondly, people were not aware of these things previously and now they feel that they should also contest the elections.

When HM was asked to comment upon who would contest for President's position next time. He replied:

> *"It is difficult to say as I cannot even convince a five year old boy nowadays this was not the case earlier. Earlier if village elders said something, others followed without any objection. Further, there have been problems among brothers (meaning Mangalars) and other people also"*

Thus, it seems to be true that there have been differences among Mangalar clan particularly between TM and HM on many issues. Some other respondents also confirmed this. It may be pertinent to observe the challenges to dominance of Kallar coming from within and not from outside the caste.

7) TRANSFORMATION OF POWER : AN OVERVIEW

Before independence, in Pudukkottai state land and social ranking constituted sources of power. Based on these sources local authorities like Ambalars and Miracidars acted as a link between the king and the village for collection of revenue and maintaining social order. With the introduction of offices of Maniam and Karnam the role of Miracidars declined. Ambalars lost their formal authority with the merger of Pudukkottai state with the Indian Union and whatever residue of power left in the office has disappeared.

With the introduction of Panchayati Raj institutions and Co-operatives, universal adult franchise and party politics, new sources of power have emerged not necessarily replacing all the earlier ones. However, some sources of power have gained relative importance than others. Caste structure has undergone changes where social hierarchy is not as rigid before. Local level leaders have to compromise with earlier values of social distance with and discrimination against lower castes atleast for canvassing of votes. Upper castes like Kallars and Udayars still occupy higher and important positions in the village. One of the reasons, apart from their social and economic position, is that Kallars are the largest single group and numerically dominant than other castes. Kallars are numerically less than the combined strength of all other major groups. Despite this Kallars have managed to capture all formal positions so far.

The reasons are varied. Firstly, Kallar candidates particularly Mangalar clan members alone stood and won the Panchayat elections since the first Panchayat elections. Other castes are divided and voted for one of the two candidates from Kallar caste. For this reason can be attributed to the claim of Kallars to traditional political authority in terms of original settlers status, dominance in 'Ur' panchayat, in temple activities and their strong kinship net-work and unity. Though other castes like Udayars, Konars and Gounders are socially ranked equal to Kallars they do not possess the elements which made Kallars dominant. Thus, Kallars after the emergence of new sources of power like Village Panchayat and Co-operatives have been able to capture positions in these institutions.

Kallars though politically dominant at local level have to share the economic dominance with Udayars. Earlier mainly Udayars, Chettiars, Muslims possessed most of the lands. Gradually Chettiars and Muslims sold off their lands particularly to Kallars. Land records of the revenue village indicate that Kallars increased their landhold-ing but still land-man ratio for Kallars is less than Udayars. Present day big landowners, like it was earlier, are from Udayar caste though land distribution is much more diffused.

There are trends discernible at the outset which show the way Kallars gained lands from other castes. In the first place when Chettiars were selling their lands they were mainly bought by

Kallars who were their tenants. Secondly there are cases to show that Kallars could create a condition whereby other castes were forced to sell their lands particularly to Kallars. Another dimension of economic power is that some power holders from Kallar caste have acquired lands after they assumed office and now against the same people, there are corruption charges.

While the caste structure and landholding provide for internal sources of power, institutions like Village Panchayat and Co-operatives and political parties constitute external sources of power. Being external sources, changes effected from outside the village made impact on the position of various power holders. The changes include irregularity of elections to these bodies and removing of powers particularly from Village Panchayat. In the absence of election and lack of powers to these institutions in the eighties severed or weakened the link between local level and the government. In this condition power holders with formal position in the ruling party emerged to act as middlemen between the government machinery and the local people.

Kallars, though have most of the elements of dominance to qualify as a dominant caste there are some dominant individuals within this dominant caste. In Udayallipatti Panchayat even within dominant caste only Mangalars among Kallars occupy important formal and informal positions.

For a caste to be dominant, existence of unity within that caste is considered essential by some scholars. Though in the Panchayat there have been factional fights among two groups of Kallars, they have demonstrated the solidarity of the caste so far. However, there are trends which might lead to challenging the solidarity and dominance of Kallars, particularly of Mangalars - the original settlers.

NOTES AND REFERENCES

1. Nicholas B. Dirks, *The Hollow Crown : Ethnohistory of an Indian Kingdom* (Cambridge : Cambridge University Press, 1987), pp.118-119.
2. Ibid.
3. K.R.Venkatrama Ayyar(ed.), *A Manual of the Pudukkottai State* Vol.I (Pudukkottai : Sri Brihadamba State Press, 1938), pp.375-378.
4. *Report on District Revenue and General Administration* Administrative Reforms Commission, (Madras : Government of Tamil Nadu, 1973).
5. The first person status of Ambalars is not always uncontested one. Some respondents informed that this position was contested by TM who was the trustee of the Veerapondor temple in the middle of the eighties against the tradition of giving prasadam first to Ambalar. However it was resolved finally to maintain status-quo. Similar incidents were reported in other areas of the district by Dirks. Nicholas B. Dirks., op.cit., pp.363-370.
6. John Harriss, *Capitalism and Peasant Farming : Agrarian Structure and Ideology in Northern Tamil Nadu* (Bombay : Oxford University Press, 1982), p.234.
7. It was reported that Kallars in the recent years have adopted new methods of creating fear among other castes about Kallars like dumping electric motors and pumps or diesel engines of their opponents in well, cutting down of crops in the nights so on.
8. This interpretation of Udayar politics was put forward by Mr.K.Nammalwar who has been working in the area for more than a decade.
9. In view of constraints of time and resource at the disposal of the researcher indepth enquiry into various aspects of economy of each household could not be carried out.
10. *The Hindu* (Madras),August 12, 1978.

11. M.N.Srinivas, *The Dominant Caste and Other Essays* (Delhi : Oxford, 1987), p.114.
12. M.N.Srinivas, "The Social System of a Mysore Village", in Mckim Marriot (ed.), *Village India* (Chicago : University of Chicago Press, 1955), p.18.
13. M.N.Srinivas, op.cit., p.114.
14. L.Dumont, *Homo Hierarchicus : An Essay on the Caste System* (Chicago : University of Chicago Press, 1980), p.162.
15. S.C.Dube, "Caste Dominance and Factionalism", *Contributions to Indian Sociology* New Series No.II, pp.58-81, 1968.
16. T.K.Oommen, "The Concept of Dominant Caste : Some Queries", *Contributions to Indian Sociology* New Series No.IV, pp.73-83, 1980 and also T.K.Oommen, *Social Structure and Politics: Studies in Independent India* (Delhi : Hinduston Publishing Corporation, 1984), pp.69-80.
17. M.N.Srinivas, op.cit., p.12.
18. S.C.Dube, op.cit., p.61.
19. M.N.Srinivas, op.cit., p.12.
20. S.C.Dube, op.cit., p.61.
21. M.N.Srinivas , op.cit., p.11.
22. T.K.Oommen, op.cit., p.72.
23. L.Dumont, op.cit., 162..
24. S.C.Dube, op.cit., p.61.
25. M.N.Srinivas, op.cit., p.12.

7 Conclusion

There are several studies on Indian villages dealing with the phenomenon of power. They have contributed to the understanding of power formation. These studies explored the nature of power formation in terms of distribution and shift of power from one section of population to the other in the changed context of introduction of adult franchise, multi-party system, Panchayati Raj and Co-operatives institutions. These studies, however, have not bestowed enough of attention on the inter-relationship between the sources of power and power holders. There is a need for studying sources of power to understand which person(s) has/have what source(s) of power and how shifts in sources of power affect the power holders.

This study aims at achieving two objectives : one to study and analyse different sources of power and also identify different power holders to understand the dynamics of power at the grass-roots level. For this purpose different sources of power such as caste structure, landholding, caste-wise landownership and manning of statutory institutions like Village Panchayat, Co-operatives and also the political parties are studied ; two, analyse the inter-relationship between sources of power and power holders. This involves studying the process of acquisition and exercise of power by different power holders, changes in the sources of power and their impact on various power holders.

The concept of power, as already pointed out, is central to the present study. Power like influence and authority has many definitions and so also application. The definitions by various scholars have not been broad enough so as to subsume all aspects of power. While some emphasised on individualistic aspect, others on institutional aspect of power. Some interpret power relations in terms of conflict and others in terms of consensus. While some conceptions of power stress on imposing one's will or affecting others behaviour despite resistance, the others on willing compliance. The present study defines power as a capacity of person or persons or groups to affect others behaviour with or without resistance in a system of social relationship, institutional framework and socio-economic structure.

To achieve the objectives of the study qualitative and quantitative data were collected. Both these data were gathered from primary and secondary sources. The primary sources include semi-structured indepth interviews, individual and group discussions and participant observation. The researcher met a cross section of people to get an insight into the phenomenon. The secondary sources include materials from books, articles, journals and newspaper clippings, district gazetteers, land records, census reports and so on.

For the purpose of the study Udayallipatti Panchayat in Pudukkottai district in Tamil Nadu has been selected. This district and the village selected shared certain general characteristics of the state in terms of population, caste composition and economic factors. It is hoped that the conclusions drawn will have wider validity.

From the analysis of different sources of power, the study of Udayallipatti Panchayat reveals that Kallars- the largest single group - were able to acquire and retain power at the village level. Other castes, though possess more than fifty percent of votes and population have not been able to contain this powerful community even in the case of Panchayats where power is acquired through electoral politics where the numbers do count. Kallars not only have captured and retained formal political power in Udayallipatti Panchayat but also in most of the Panchayats of the Kunnondorkoil

Panchayat Union. The Kallars of the area were able to win in 25 out of total 38 Panchayats. This indicates that it is not the particular caste that is the critical source of power at the village level. On the contrary the source of power is located in the kinship network and solidarity of a particular caste on the one hand and division and differentiation among different castes in the village on the other.

That Kallars derive their power from inter-caste distance of other castes is obvious from the data. Though socially Kallars are placed on par with Udayars, Gounders and Konars, the latter lack sufficient strength and unity among themselves to challenge Kallars. On the contrary they are dependent on Kallars in solving both inter-caste and intra-caste disputes. Kallars are not only approached by other castes but the former retain initiative and take a lead on their own in dealing with the caste disputes or differences arising from time to time.

Apart from dominating 'Ur' panchayat, the Kallars dominate temple activities of the village : all the trustees of the main temple in recent years belong to Kallar caste and particularly from Mangalar clan. In the main temple, Ambalar from Kallar caste is given 'prasadam' first as a recognition of his status and also status of his caste. Generally Kallars take lead in conducting festivals in most of the temples of the village. The relationship between the temple and power has been one of the old linkages in South Indian power structure. Religious institutions and political power have had the mechanism of reinforcing each other. The continuation of these linkages and the process is noticed at micro-level in the village till to-day.

Kallars share the economic dominance particularly the land with Udayars. Earlier, mainly Udayars, Chettiars, Muslims possessed most of the lands. Gradually Chettiars and Muslims sold off their lands mostly to Kallars. Land records of the revenue village indicate that Kallars succeeded in increasing their landholding but still land-man ratio for Kallars is less than Udayars. Present day big landowners, as the case was earlier, are from Udayar caste though land distribution is much more diffused.

There are trends discernible which show the way Kallars gained lands from other castes. In the first place when Chettiars were selling their lands they were mainly bought by Kallars who were their tenants. Secondly, there are cases to show that Kallars could create conditions whereby other castes were forced to sell their lands particularly to Kallars. Another dimension of economic power is that some power holders from Kallar caste have acquired lands and reportedly, there are corruption charges against them. These power holders when they acquired power they did not own as much lands as they do now. This indicates that while economic power like landholding facilitates acquisition of political power, it is equally true that political power can help in acquisition of economic power.

The Kallars, it is evident from the study, command both formal and informal power. Formal power includes hold over administrative and developmental activities and informal power includes the social influence and linkages with the world outside the village. As a part of this phenomenon one can see the hold of Kallars over the Panchayat and Co-operative institutions on the one hand and the AIADMK party on the other. A Kallar is Union Secretary to AIADMK which was in power at the state level. While the hold over local institutions help the Kallars to consolidate their power, the party linkages help for its further reinforcement.

The above details are useful to identify power holders. But an analysis of individual power holders in terms of their profiles and sources of power would also be equally useful for this analysis. Therefore, an attempt is made to compare the socio-economic background of power holders. It is found that most of them in addition to belonging to the Kallar upper caste, they are cultivators and middle aged. Their educational achievement is not impressive. In addition to their own support structure at the village level, their linkages with the outside power structure also play an important role. It would be, however, rewarding if an indepth analysis of their personal traits is done.

In terms of inter-relationship the study indicates that before independence, in Pudukkottai state, land and social ranking constituted the real sources of power. Based on these sources local authorities like Ambalars and Miracidars acted as a link between the king and the village for collection of revenue and maintaining social order. With the introduction of offices of Maniam and Karnam the role of Miracidars declined. Ambalars almost lost their formal authority with the merger of Pudukkottai state with the Indian Union.

With the introduction of institutions of Panchayati Raj and Co-operatives, universal adult franchise and party politics, there emerged new sources of power but not necessarily replacing all the earlier forms. Some sources of power gained relatively more importance than others. Caste structure underwent changes in terms of hierarchical rigidities. Local level leaders made compromises on earlier practices like social distance with and discrimination against lower castes. That is how Kallars have been able to retain the power. However, the compromises made by Kallars in caste relationships are more in the form and ritualistic than in the real content and essence of the caste.

The study reveals that Kallar candidates particularly of Mangalar clan won the Panchayat elections. Though other castes like Udayars, Konars and Gounders are socially ranked equal to Kallars, they do not possess certain elements which made Kallars dominant. While numerical strength of Kallars did help them, the other castes are so divided that they had voted for one of the two Kallar candidates. An important reason seems to be the claim of Kallars to traditional political authority in terms of original settlers status. Thus, Kallars had the advantage in capturing the new sources of power like Village Panchayat and Co-operatives.

While the caste structure and landholding provide internal sources of power, institutions like Village Panchayat, Co-operatives and political parties, as pointed out, constitute external sources of power. Being external sources, changes effected from outside the village do make a difference on the position of power holders. The changes include absence of periodic elections and lack of powers to these institutions in the eighties, the link between local level and the government got weakened. In this condition power holders with formal position in the ruling party got transformed as middlemen between the government machinery and the local people. The power holders hailing from the Kallar community have been able to perform this role of middlemen with considerable ease.

The study on power dynamics reveals that at the grass-roots level caste which is capable of developing internal solidarity and kinship network can not only capture the power but retain it. This seems to have played more important role than the landownership. In the changed context capturing formal institutions of power, in addition to retaining the traditional cultural linkages with religious institutions, has come to assume considerable importance. In the absence of formal institutions, the power holders are reduced into middlemen. As they have struck linkages with the outside power structure, they are able to consolidate and also use the linkages for further reinforcement of their power. The castes like Kallar caste seems to be not only endowed with certain internal characteristics but are able to retain power through self adjustment to the changing situation. Thus one perceived not a qualitative change in the social base of power but certain changes in the forms and processes of power.

Bibliography

Aiyar,S.R., *A General History of Pudukkottai State* (Pudukkottai : Sri Brihadamba Press, 1916)

Ayyar, K.R.V.(ed.), *A Manual of the Pudukkottai State Vol. I Part I* (Pudukkottai : Sri Brihadamba Press, 1940)

_________, *A Manual of the Pudukkottai State Vol.I* (Pudukkottai: Sri Brihadamba Press, 1938)

Bailey, F.G., *Caste and Economic Frontier: A Village in Highland Orissa* (Bombay : Oxford, 1958)

Baker,C.J., *The Politics of South India,1920-1936*(Cambridge : The University Press, 1975)

_____________, *An Indian Rural Economy 1880-1955 : The Tamil Nadu Countryside* (Delhi : Oxford, 1984)

Balandiar, G., *Political Anthropology*(Harmondsworth : Penguin, 1972)

Barnes, B., *The Nature of Power* (Chicago : The University of Illinois Press, 1988)

Barnett, M.R., *The Politics of Cultural Nationalism in South India* (NewJersey:PrincetonUniveristy Press, 1976)

Bell.R.et.al., *Political Theory : A Reader in Theory and and Research* (New York · The Free Press 1969)

Berg, Bruce., *Qualitative Research Methods for Social Sciences* (Boston : Allyn and Bacon, 1984)

Beteille, A., *Caste, Class and Power: Changing Patterns of Social Stratification in Tanjore Village* (London : University of California Press, 1971)

______________, *Caste: Old and New, Essays in Social Structure and Social Stratification* (Bombay : Asia Publishing House, 1969)

______________, *Studies in Agrarian Social Structure* (Delhi : Oxford, 1974)

______________, *Inequality and Social Change* (Bombay : Oxford University, 1985)

______________, *Inequality Among Men* (Oxford : Basil Blackwell, 1977)

Blackburn, R.(ed.), *Ideology in Social Science*(Glasgow : Fontana, 1979)

Bhatt, A., *Caste, Class and Politics* (New Delhi : Manohar, 1975)

Bogdon, R. and Taylor, S.T., *Introduction to Qualitative Research Methods: A Phenomenological Approach to the Social Sciences* (New york : John Wiley, 1975)

Brauss, P.R., *Factional Politics in Indian State: The Congress Party in Uttar Pradesh* (Bombay : Oxford University Press, 1960)

Bryman, A., *Quantity and Quality in Social Research* (London : Unwin Hyman, 1988)

Burgess, R. G., *In the Field: An Introduction to Field Research* (London : Unwin Hyman, 1989)

Campbell, Tom., *Seven Theories of Human Society* (Oxford : Clarendon Press, 1981)

Chaudary, S.N., *Dynamics of Rural Power Structure: A Case Study of an Indian Village* (Delhi : Amar Prakashan, 1987)

Chaudhuri, K.N. and Clive J.D.(eds.), *Economy and Society: Essays in Indian Economic and Social History* (New Delhi : Oxford, 1979)

Clegg, S.R., *Power, Rule and Domination: A Critical and Empir-*

ical Understanding of Power in Sociological Theory and Organisational Life (London : Routledge and Kegan Paul, 1975)

__________, *Frameworks of Power* (Delhi : Sage, 1989)

Desai,A.R., *Rural Sociology in India* (Bombay : Popular Prakashan, 1978

Dahl,Robert,A., *Democracy and Power in an American city* (New Haven : Yale University Press, 1961)

Dharampal, *The Madras Panchayat System : A Historical Survey* Vol I (Delhi : Impex India, 1972)

Dirks,N.B., *The Hollow Crown: Ethnohistory of an Indian Kingdom* (Bombay : Orient Longman, 1989)

Djurfeldt,G. and Lindberg,S., *Behind Poverty: The Social Formation in a Tamil Village* (Bombay : Oxford and IBHD, 1975)

Dumont, Louis., *Homo Hierarchicus: An essay on the Caste System* (Chicago : The Univeristy of Chicago, 1970)

__________, *Religion, Politics and History in India* (Paris : Mouton, 1970)

__________ , *A South Indian Sub-Caste: Social Organisation and Religion of the Pramalai Kallars* (Delhi : Oxford University Press, 1986)

Duverger, M., *Introduction to the Social Sciences* (London : George Allen and Unwin, 1964)

Epstein, T.S., *Economic Development and Social Change in South India* (Bombay : Oxford University Press, 1962)

Frankel,F.R., *India's Political Economy 1947-1977: The Gradual Revolution* (Delhi : Oxford University Press, 1984)

Frankel,F.R.and Rao, M.S.A. (eds.), *Dominance and State Power in Modern India: Decline of a Social Order Vol. I* (Delhi Oxford, 1989)

Gandhimathi,V., *Community, Authority and Power in Social Thought: A Philosophical Analysis* (Poona : Thesis submitted to University of Poona, 1982)

Gangadere, K.D., *Emerging Patterns of leadership* (Delhi : Rachna, 1974)

Garratt. G.T., *The legacy of India* (Oxford : Clarendon Press, 1951)

Ghuraye. G.S., *Caste and Race in India* (Bombay : Popular Prakashan, 1963)

Giddens, A. and Held,D. (eds.),*Classes, Power and Conflicts : Classical and Contemporary Debates* (Hampshire : Macmillan, 1982)

Gough, K., *Rural Society in South-East India* (Cambridge : The Cambridge University Press, 1974)

__________, *Rural Change in South East India,1950s to 1980s* (Delhi : Oxford, 1989)

Gould, H.A., *Politics and Caste* (Delhi : Chanakya, 1990)

Grover, V., *Elections and Politics in India* (New Delhi : Deep and Deep, 1988)

Habib,Irfan.,*Caste and Money in Indian History* (Bombay : University of Bombay, 1987)

Hardgrave,R.L.,*The Dravidian Movement* (Bombay : Popular Prakashan, 1965)

Harichandran,C.,*Panchayati Raj and Rural Development : A Study of Tamil Nadu* (New Delhi : Concept, 1983)

Harriss, J., *Capitalism and Peasant Farming: Agrarian Structure and Ideology in Northern Tamil Nadu* (Bombay : Oxford, 1982)

Hobsbawn E.J. (ed.), *Peasants in History: Essays in Honour of Daniel Thornier* (Calcutta : Oxford, 1980)

Hunter,F.,*Community Power Structure* (Chapel Hill : University of North Carolina Press, 1953)

Irschide,E.F., *Politics and Social conflict in South India: The Non-Brahmin Movement and Tamil Separatism 1916-1924* (California : California University Press, 1969)

Iyengar, P.T.S., *History of the Tamils from the earliest times to 600 A.D.* (Delhi : Asian Educational Services, 1983)

Karuppaiyan,V., *Kinship and Polity : A Study in Socio-Political Organisation among the Upland Kallars of Thanjavur district in Tamil Nadu*(Madras : University of Madras, 1990)

Kashyap,A., *Panchayati Raj: Views of the Founding Fathers and Recommendations of Different Committees* (New Delhi : Lancer Books, 1989)

Kipnis,d., *The Power Holders* (Chicago : The University of Chicago Press, 1976)

Kohli,Atul., *The State and Poverty in India: The Politics of Reforms* (Cambridge : Cambridge University Press, 1987)

__________, *Indian Democracy: An Analysis of Changing State-Society Relationship* (New Jersey : Princeton University Press, 1988)

Kosambi, D.D., *The Culture and Civilisation of Ancient India in Historical Outline* (Delhi : Vikas, 1981)

Kothari, R. (ed.), *Caste in Indian Politics* (New Delhi : Orient Longman, 1970)

Krishna,G.(ed.), *Contributions to South Asian Studies Vol.I* (Delhi: Oxford University Press, 1979)

Kumar, D., *Land and Caste in South India* (Camb idge : The Univeristy Press, 1965)

Kumar,S. and Venkatraman,K., *State-Panchayati Raj Relations: Study of Supervision and Control in Tamil Nadu* Bombay : Asia, 1974)

Kurian C.J., *Dynamics of Rural Transformation: A Study of Tamil Nadu1950-1975* (Madras : Orient Longman, 1981)

Lenoy,Richard., *The Speaking Tree: A Study of Indian Culture* (Delhi: Oxford, 1971)

Lincoln, S.Y. and Cuba,G.E., *Naturalistic Inquiry* (New Delhi : Sage, 1985)

Ludden, David., *Peasant History in South India* (Delhi : Oxford University Press, 1989)

Lukes, Steven., *Power: A Radical view* (London : Macmillan, 1974)

Mahalingam,T.V., *Readings in South Indian History* (Delhi : B.R, 1976)

Mandelbaum,D.G., *Society in India: Volumes I & II* (Bombay : Popular Prakashan, 1972)

Marriott, M., *Village India: Studies in the Little Community* (Chicago : University of Chicago Press, 1955)

Martin, R., *The Sociology of Power* (New Delhi : Ambika, 1978)

Mathrubutham,R.and Srinivasan,R., *The Madras Village Panchayats Act, 1950* (Madras : Law Journal Office, 1958)

Mencher, J.P., *Agriculture and Social Structure in Tamil Nadu: Past Origins, Present Transformation and Future Prospects* (Delhi : Allied, 1978)

Miller,R., *Analysing Marx: Morality, Power and History* (New Jersey : Princeton University, 1984)

Mohapatra,J.K., *Factional Politics in India* (Allahabad : Chugh, 1985)

Moore, B., *Social Origins of Dictatorship and Democracy : Lord and Peasant in the Making of Modern World* (London : Penguin, 1987)

_________ , *Political Power and Social Theory* (Massachutts : Harward University, 1984)

Muthayya, M.B.L., *Panchayat Union Administration* (Tamil) (Madras : New Century, 1986)

__________, *District Development Council* (Tamil)(Madras : New Century, 1987)

Narain,I.(ed.), *State Politics in India* (Meerat : Meenakshi, 1976)

Ng,Sik Hung., *The Social Psychology of Power* (London : Academic Press, 1980)

Olsen,M. (ed.), *Power in Societies* (London : Collier Macmillan, 1970)

Oommen, T.K., *Social Structure and Politics in Independent India* (Delhi : Hindustan Publishing Corporation, 1984)

Pandey, B.N.(ed.), *Leadership in South Asia* (New Delhi : Vikas, 1977)

Pandian,M.S.S., *The Image Trap : M. G. Ramachandran in Films and Politics* (New Delhi : Sage, 1992)

Park,R.L.and Tinker,J., *Leadership and Political Institutions in India* (Madras : Oxford University Press, 1960)

Parpola,A.and Hansen,B.S.,*South Asian Religion and Society* (New Delhi : D.K., 1986)

Parry,G.,*Political Elites* (London: George Allen and Unwin Ltd, 1969)

Parsons,T., *Sociological Theory and Modern Society* (New york : Free Press, 1967)

Patton,M.Q., *Qualitative Evaluation and Research Methods* (Delhi : Sage, 1990)

Pillai,S.D(ed.), *Aspects of changing India: Studies in Honour of Prof.G.S.Ghurye* (Bombay : Popular Prakashan, 1976)

Polsby, N.W.,*Community Power and Political Theory*(New Haven: Yale University press, 1963)

Poulantzas,N., *Political Power and Social Classes* (London : New Left Books, 1973)

Prasad, V.S., *Panchayats and Development* (New Delhi : Light and Life, 1981)

Pughazhenthi,S.,*Panchayats,Town Panchayats and Panchayat Unions : Law and Practice* (Tamil) (Madras : Poongodi, 1990)

Rajasekhariah,A.M.,*Religion and Politics in India-Two Models of Hindu Society and Their Political Implications* (Madras : Univeristy of Madras, 1981)

Ramachandran,K.S.(ed.), *Readings in South Indian History* (Delhi : B.R., 1977)

Ram Reddy.G.(ed.), *Patterns of Panchayati Raj in India* (Madras : Macmillan, 1977)

Ranga Rao, K., *Village Politics: A longitudinal study* (Bombay : Popular Prakashan, 1980)

Rudolph,L. and Rudolph,S.H., *The Modernity of Tradition: Political Development in India* (Chicago : The University Press, 1967)

Russell,B., *Power: A New Social Analysis* (London : Unwin Books, 1960)

Sankarankutty,T.P(ed.),*Modern India: Society and Politics in Transition* (New Delhi : Inter India, 1988)

Saraswathi,S., *The Madras Panchayat System, Volume I: A Historical Survey* (Delhi : Impex India, 1973)

Sastri,K.A.N., *A History of South India* (Madras:Oxford University Press, 1987)

Satyanathan, A.N.,*The Dravidian Movement in Tamil Nadu and its Legacy* (Madras : University of Madras, 1982)

Schwarzmantel,J.J.,*Structure of Power: An Introduction to Politics* (Sussex : Wheat Sheaf Books, 1987)

Shakir, M., *Religion, State and Politics in India* (Delhi : Ajantha, 1989)

Sherring, M.A.,*Tribes and Castes of Madras Presidency* (Delhi : Cosmo, 1975)

Singer,M.and Bernard,C.(eds.), *Structure and Change in Indian Society* (Chicago : Aldeni, 1968)

Singh,V.B.and Bose,S., *State Elections in India: Data Hand book On Vidhan Sabha Elections,1952-1985 Vol-5* (New Delhi: Sage, 1988)

Sinha,M.M.,*Community Power Structure in Rural India: A Study of Two Villages in Bihar(India)* (New York : Unpublished thesis from Cornell University, 1974)

Siversten, D., *When Caste Barriers fall: A Study of Social and Economic Change in a South Indian Village* (Nowny : George Allen and Unwin, 1963)

Smith,D.E (ed.),*South Asian Politics and Religion* (New Jersey : Princeton University Press, 1969)

Sparatt, P., *D.M.K in Power* (Bombay : Nachiketa, 1970)

Spear,P., *A History of India Vol.II* (Harmondsworth : Penguin, 1981)

Srinivas,M.N., *Religion and Society among the Coorgs of South India* (Bombay : MPP, 1978)

________, *The Remembered village* (Delhi : Oxford University, 1979)

________, *Social Change in Modern India* (Delhi : Orient Longman, 1984)

________(ed.), *India's Villages* (Bombay : MPP, 1985)

________, *The Dominant caste and Other Essays* (Delhi : Oxford, 1987)

________, *Caste in Modern India*(Bombay : MPP, 1989)

________, *The Cohesive Rcle of Sanskritization and Other Essays* (Delhi : Oxford, 1989)

Stein, Burton.,*Peasant State and Society in Medieval South India* (Delhi : Oxford, 1985)

Strauss, A.L., *Qualitative Analysis for Social Scientists* (New York : Cambridge, 1989)

Thapar,R., *A History of India Vol.I* (Harmondsworth : Penguin, 1982)

Thurston,E (ed.),*Castes and Tribes of Southern India, Volume I to VI* (Delhi : Cosmos, 1975)

Venkatesan, G., *Development of Rural Local Self Government* (Coimbatore : Rainbow; 1983)

Vidyarthy,L.P.(ed.), *Leadership in India* (New Delhi : Asia Publishing House, 1967)

Washbrook, D.A.,*The Emergence of Provincial Politics: The Madras Presidency,1870-1920* (New Delhi : Vikas, 1977)

Weiner,M.and John,O.F. (eds.), *Electoral Politics in the Indian States: Party System and Cleavages Volume I*(Delhi : Manohar, 1975)

Wiser, W.H.,*The Hindu Jajmani System* (Lucknow : Lucknow Publishing House, 1969)

Wolfinger, R.E., *Readings in American Political Behaviour*(Engelwood Cliffs : Prentice Hall, 1970)

Wrong,D.H., *Power: Its Forms, Bases and Uses* (Basil Black Well : Oxford, 1979).

GOVERNMENT PUBLICATIONS

Census of India 1931, 1951 to 1991.

District Development Councils Act 1958 (Madras : Government of Tamil Nadu, 1959)

G.O MS.No 790 dated 21-10-1985, (Madras : Rural Development Department, Government of Tamil Nadu, 1985)

G.O MS.No 13 dated 18-1-1986 (Madras : Rural Development Department, Government of Tamil Nadu, 1986)

Pudukkottai District Gazetteer (Madras : Government of Tamil Nadu, 1988)

Report on District Revenue and General Administration (Madras : Administrative Reforms Commission, Government of Tamil Nadu, 1973)

The Tamil Nadu Co-operative Societies Act, 1961 (Madras : Government of Tamil Nadu, 1980)

The Tamil Nadu Co-operative Societies Rules, 1963 (Madras : Government of Tamil Nadu, 1980)

The Tamil Nadu Panchayats Act, 1958 (Madras : Government of Tamil Nadu, 1959)

Tamil Nadu Public Service Commission Bulletin (Madras : Government of Tamil Nadu, 1989)

ARTICLES

Abraham, C.M., "A Review of the Trends in the Caste System", *MIDS Bulletin* 9(12), December,1979, pp.59-89.

Bahrach,P and Baratz,M.S.,"The Two Faces of Power", *American Political Science Review* 50, 1962, pp.947-52.

Baskaran, S. Theodore., "Music for the Masses : Film Songs of Tamil Nadu", *Economic and Political Weekly* (Annual number) March 1991, pp 755-758.

Bhowmik, S.K.,"Caste and Class in India", *Economic and Political Weekly* 27(24&25), June 1992, pp.1246- 1248.

Chattopadhyay,S.N., "Historical context of Political Change in Rural West Bengal A Study of Six villages in West Bengal",*Economic and Political Weekly* XXVII (13), March 28, 1992, pp. 647-658.

Deshpande,V.N.,"Some Methodological issues in the study of Caste and Class in the Indian/Rural Social Structure", *MIDS Bulletin* 9 (12), 1979, pp.107-138.

Dirks, Nicholas,B.,"The Structure and Meaning of Political Relations in a South Indian Little Kingdom",*Contributions to Indian Sociology* 13(2), 1979, pp 169-206.

________, "The pasts of Palaiyakarar: The Ethnohistory of a South Indian Little Kingdom", *Journal of Asian Studies* XLI(4), August 1982, pp 655 -683.

________, "The Original Caste: Power, History and Hierarchy in South Asia", *Contributions to Indian Sociology* 23(1), 1989, pp. 59-77.

Dube, S.C.,"Caste Dominance and Factionalism",*Contributions to Indian Sociology* New Series No.II, 1968, pp.58-61.

Forrester V.D.,"Factions and Filmstars: Tamil Nadu Politics since 1971", *Asian Survey* XVI(3), 1976, pp. 283-296.

Gabriel, S.,"Social Background to Politics in Tamil Nadu", *The Indian Journal of Political Studies* 2(1), January 1978, pp 176-182.

Gaidern,Peter M.,"Dominance in India: A Reappraisal", *Contributions to Indian Sociology* New Series No.II, 1968, pp.82-97.

Gebert,Rita,"Poverty Alleviation and Village Politics in Tamil Nadu: Whose Interests first", *Economic and Political Weekly* XXIV(4), January 28, 1989, pp.197-202.

Gould, H.A., "The Adoptive Functions of Caste in Contemporary Indian Society", *Asian Survey* III(119), September 1963, pp 544-559.

Goyal, D.P., "Caste and Politics : A Conceptual Framework", *Asian Survey* V(10), October 1965, pp. 522-252.

Gupta, N.K., "Political Development and Political Leadership in Village Communities", *Indian Journal of Social Research* XXV(2), August 1984, Pp. 181-192.

Haragopal, G., and Balaramulu, Ch., "The Social Background of Administrative and Political Elite in Panchayati Raj: Cause for tension",*The Indian Journal of Political Science* XXXIX (2), April-June, 1978, pp.299-305.

Hardgrave, Robert L., "The riots in Tamil Nadu", Problems and Prospects of India language crisis", *Asian Survey* V(8), August 1965, pp 399-407.

________, "Politics and the Film in Tamil Nadu: The Stars and the D.M.K", *Asian Survey* III(3). March 1973, pp.288- 305.

Hirway, I.,"Panchayati Raj at Cross Roads", *Economic andPolitical Weekly* XXIV(29), 22 July 1989, pp. 1663 - 1667.

Macdougall,J.,"Dominant Caste or Rich Peasants?", *Economic and Political Weekly* XIV(12 & 13), 24 March 1979,

pp. 625 - 634.

__________, *"Two models of Power in Contemporary Rural India"*, Contributions to Indian Sociology 14(1), 1980, pp 77-94.

Manivannan,R., *"1991 Tamil Nadu Elections- Issues, Strategies and Performance"*, *Economic and Political Weekly* XXVII(4), January 25, 1992, pp. 164-170.

Menon, Mukundan C., "Tamil Nadu Election: How the Communists fared", *Economic and Political Weekly* XXIV (11),18 March 1989, pp. 549-550.

Nair K.F., "Factions and Kinship: The Case of a South Indian Village", *Asian Survey* XVI (12), December 1976, pp. 1136-1150.

Neale, W.C., "Indian Community Development, Local Government, Local Planning and Rural Policy since 1950", *Economic Development and Cultural Change* 33(4), July 1985, pp. 677-698.

Oommen, T.K., "The Concept of Dominant Caste: Some Queries", *Contributions to Indian Sociology* New Series No.IV, 1980, pp 73-83.

Pandian, M.S.S.,"Culture and Subaltern Consciousness :an aspect of MGR Phenomenon", *Economic and Political Weekly* XXIV (30),July 29 1989,pp. 759-770.

__________, "Parasakthi: Life and Time of a DMK Film", *Economic and Political Weekly* (AnnualNumber) March 1991, pp 759-770.

__________,and Geeta, V., "Jayalalitha : Sworn Heir", *Economic and Political Weekly* XXIV(11), March 18, 1989, p. 551.

Perumal,C.A.and Thandavan,R.,"Regional Parties of Tamil Nadu: A Case Study of AIADMK", *The Indian Journal ofPolitical Studies* 6&7 (1), July 1987, pp. 31-39.

Radhakrishnan,P.,"Backward Classes in Tamil Nadu 1872-1988", *Economic and Political Weekly* XXV (10), March 10, 1990, pp. 509-520.

Raheja, G.G., "India: Caste, Kingship and Dominance Reconsidered", *Annual Review of Anthropology* 17, 1988, pp. 497-552 and July 1989, pp 62 - 68.

Sathyamurthy,T.V., "Tamil Nadu Assembly Elections: Problems and Prospects", *Economic and Political Weekly* XXIV (16), April 22, 1989, pp.883-892.

Schwartz, M.S.and Scwartz,C.G.,"Problems in Participant Observation", *American Journal of Sociology* 60(4). 1955, pp.343-353.

Seth, V.N.,"Critical Review of major trends in Caste studies in India", *Indian Journal of Social Studies* 28(4), 1987, pp.373-392.

Sharma, M.L., "Rural Politics in Rajasthan: A Study of the interaction Patterns of Caste, Class and Power", *Political Science Review* 16 (3-4), 1977, pp.62-79.

Sharma, S.P., "A Materialist Thesis on the Origin and Continuity of the Caste System in South Asia",

Eastern Anthropologist 36(1), 1983, pp.55-77.

Singh,P., "Caste as a determinant of Rural Leadership: A case study of Haryana", *Indian Political Science Review* 7(2), 1983, pp. 157-162.

Singh, Y.,"Review of studies on Caste and Class in India",

Indian Journal of Social Research 29(1), 1988 pp.15-30.

Srinivas,M.N.,"Some Reflections on the nature of Caste Hierarchy", *Contributions to Indian Sociology* 18(2), 1984, pp.151-167

Stern, H., "Power in Modern India Caste or Class: An Approach and Case Study", *Contributions to Indian Sociology* 13(1), 1979, pp. 61-84.

Thandhavan, R.,"AIADMK in Tamil Nadu: Its Emergence and Unprecedented Growth", *The Indian Journal of Political Studies* 9, December 1985, pp 53-85.

Vidyasagar, R., "Vanniyars Agitation", *Economic and Political Weekly* XXIII(11), March 12 1988, pp. 507-511.

Index

Ambalar, 135, 149
Asaris, 72

Bahrach, P, 6
Bailey, F.G., 1, 8
Baratz, M.S., 6
Beals, Alan R., 8
Beteille, Andra, 1, 9, 88, 93, 100
Bhatta, A., 10
Bryman, Allan, 73

Chethar, Palaniappa, 135
Clagg, Stewart R., 5
Cooperatives, 45–46, 106–07

Dahl, Robert A., 3–6
Dirks, Nicolas B., 71, 135
Dube, S.C., 88, 149–51
Dumont, L., 88, 99, 149–50

Gardener, Peter M., 88
Gough, Kathleen, 1
Gounders, 72

Harriss, John, 1, 10, 141
Hunter, Floyd, 5

Idaiyars, 39–40
Indian rural society, 1–24
  British administration on, 1
  Limitations of study, 19–20
  Methodological framework, 12–19
  Need for study on, 11–12
  Objectives of study, 12, 157–58
  Review of literature, 7–11
  Theoretical framework of, 2–7
    Power, 2–7

Jayalalitha, 46
Jeewan Thera' Scheme, 126
Jenninga, M.K., 5

Kakhan, 116
Kallars, 37–38, 67–69
Kammalas, 39
Kamraj, 116
Karuppayan, V., 99
Konars, 70

Landholding pattern, 99–103
  Caste and, 99–102
  Categories of, 102–03
  Power formation and, 144–46
Lukes, Steven, 6

Mangalar, Duraiswamy, 135
Mencher, Joan P., 92, 103
Methodological framework, 12–19, 158
  Data collection and analysis, 14–19
  Types of data and their sources, 12–14
Moopnar, G. K., 70

Oommen, T.K., 10, 11, 149, 150

Pallars and Paraiyars (SC), 39, 71–72
Panchayat system, 40–45
Parsons, T., 3
Patton, M. Q., 13
Polsby, N.W., 5, 6
Power, 2–7
  Decision-making, 5–7
  Definitions, 2–5, 158
  Sources of, 87–112
Power holders, 113–33, 160
  B. M. profile, 122–23
  Comparative analysis of, 128–32
  H M profile, 114–17
  K M A profile, 126
  KSV profile, 124–25
  PHP profile, 126
  PNM profile, 123–24
  Power formation, 113–14
  Q N profile, 114–17
  SBS profile, 126–28
  SP profile, 121–22
  TM profile, 119–20
  TSO profile, 125
  WMR profile, 120–21
Powlantzas, N., 3
Pudukkottai district–Tamil Nadu, 11, 25–53
  Agriculture development, 28–30, 49
  Area of, 26
  Historical background of, 26–28, 49
  Industrial development, 34
  Irrigation development, 30–34
  Physiography and ecology, 28, 50
  Political parties performance in Assembly elections, 46–49, 50
  Population of, 25–26, 34–40 50
    Caste composition, 34–36
    Caste groups, 37–40
    Religions groups, 40
  Rural institutions, 40–46
    Co-operatives, 45–46
    Panchayat institutions, 40–45, 49
Pusaris, 70–71

Raju, V., 127
Ramachandran, Janaki, 46
Ramachandran, M.G., 46
Rammaya, 116

Saybu, Babar Khan, 130
Schattschneiders, 6
Sharma, S.S., 10
Singh, Y, 9
Sinha, M.M., 10
Sri Veerapondor Temple, 74, 119
Srinivas, M.N., 1, 88, 96, 149–51
Swamy, S.B., 127

Theoretical framework, 2–7
Power, 2–7
Thirunauvkarasu, 5, 119
Transfer of power, 134–56, 161–62
Caste structure and power formation, 136–44, 161
Dominant persons within dominant caste, 149–50
Emerging trends, 151–52
Factionalism and power formation, 150–51
Institutions, party politics and power formation, 146–48
Land holding and power formation, 144–46
Overview of, 152–54

Udayallipatti, Panchayat, 54–86, 158
Agriculture and Irrigation, 57–60, 84
Caste and land holding, 76–78, 84
Caste groups and structure, 67–74
Institutions, 79–82, 85
Co-operative, 81
Others, 82
Panchayats, 79–81
Landholding categories, 79
Location and ecology of, 55–57
Party politics, 82–84
People of, 60–67
Literacy level, 60–61
Occupational pattern, 61–67
Population, 60
Religions groups and their activities, 74–76
Settlement pattern, 62–63, 84
Udayallipatti, Panchayat—Sources of power, 87–112, 158
Caste structure, 82–99, 108–09, 158
Inter-caste relationship, 94–98, 109, 159
Kinship network, 99
Numerical strength, 88–94, 158–59
Landholding pattern, 99–103, 159–60
Political institutions, 103–08, 160
Co-operatives, 106–07
Party parties, 107–08, 110
Village panchayats, 103–06
Udayar caste, 38, 69–70
Udayar, M. K., 125, 135, 139, 143, 146

Valayars, 38–39, 69–70
Veerappan, R.M., 119, 120, 148
Vishwakarma Association, 72

Walton, J., 5
Weber, 3–4
Wolfinger, R E, 5